hamlyn
wok & stir-fry

hamlyn
wok & stir-fry

Jeni Wright

a guide to quick, healthy cooking

NOTES

Standard level spoon measurements are used in all recipes

1 tablespoon = one 15 ml spoon

1 teaspoon = one 5 ml spoon

Both metric and imperial measurements
have been given in all recipes.
Use one set of measurements only
and not a mixture of both.

Eggs should be large unless otherwise stated

Pepper should be freshly ground black pepper
unless otherwise stated

Fresh herbs should be used unless otherwise stated
If unavailable use dried herbs as an alternative
but halve the quantities stated

FOR MY CHILDREN, OLIVER AND SOPHIE

First published in Great Britain in 1992 by Hamlyn
a division of Octopus Publishing Group Limited,
2–4 Heron Quays, London E14 4JP

Reprinted 1993, 1994 (twice), 1996, 1999
This paperback edition published in 2001

ISBN 0 600 60542 6

A CIP catalogue for this book is available from the British Library

Produced by Toppan, Hong Kong
Printed in China

CONTENTS

INTRODUCTION

The technique of stir-frying in a wok is simple and quick, thus making it an ideal cooking method for today's busy lifestyle. Meals can be made in moments in a wok, with the added bonus that they're nutritious too – stir-frying uses the minimum amount of fat and the speed of cooking keeps ingredients at their freshest and best, with natural goodness retained.

THE WOK

The ancient Chinese invented the wok – it has been used in the East for centuries – but now this cleverly designed pan has found its way to the West, and modern cooks have quickly

STEAMING
Using a bamboo steamer to steam fish over a wok.

discovered just how easy it is to use – and how versatile too, because it can be used for steaming, deep-frying and braising as well as stir-frying.

The secret of the wok's success lies in its unique shape: its high sides and rounded bottom allow the cook to toss and stir the food around over a high heat, so that it cooks evenly. The heat is conducted more quickly in a wok than in a conventionally shaped pan, so that ingredients cook in the minimum amount of time, retaining their natural colour and flavour. Vegetables keep their crispness, fish its shape and texture, while meat and poultry are beautifully juicy and tender. Only a very small amount of oil is needed for cooking – just enough to swirl around the bottom of the pan – and because only top-quality, lean meat is used, food stir-fried in a wok is generally low in fat and cholesterol – and calories too.

The wok is suited to most occasions, from family meals in a hurry, when your eye is forever glancing at the kitchen clock, to informal entertaining, where your guests can watch you tossing and turning the ingredients on top of the cooker.

CHOOSING A WOK

A conventional frying pan can be used for stir-frying, as long as it is heavy-based, but traditional Chinese woks are so inexpensive that it hardly seems worth managing without one – no other pan conducts heat quite so well and has the unique shape that enables you to stir and toss the ingredients up the sides.

There is a huge variety of woks available. Some come in boxed sets together with accessories such as stands, lids and cooking utensils, but these sets may not always be a good buy, so check the contents carefully before you purchase. By far the best kind of wok is the simple, inexpensive Chinese wok which you can buy in oriental supermarkets and hardware stores. Usually made of thin carbon steel (the best conductor of heat), this kind of wok has a round bottom and deep, sloping sides. Avoid buying woks made of stainless steel as they do not conduct heat well. Non-stick woks are a Western invention and obviously not authentic, but they work quite well; they are easy to use – and to keep clean. Electric woks should be avoided altogether because they do not get hot enough for successful stir-frying.

Take care not to buy a wok that is too small, or you will find it difficult to stir and toss the ingredients without them falling out of the pan. The ideal sized wok is 35 cm (14 inches) in diameter, which allows plenty of room for ingredients for 4 people. (It is short-sighted to buy a smaller wok, even if you generally cook for less than four.) A large wok also gives you more room for tossing a small amount of ingredients, which makes life much easier if you are a newcomer to stir-frying.

For stir-frying, the best wok to choose is the one-handled type, which allows you to hold the wok firmly in one hand while tossing and stirring with a metal scoop or spatula in the other. The Chinese call this a pau wok. Look for a pau wok with a wooden handle, as metal handles become too hot and stir-frying is impossibly awkward if you are wearing oven gloves. Woks with two short handles on either side are known as Cantonese woks. These types of woks are intended for steaming and deep-frying. They have slightly flatter bottoms than pau woks and are therefore more stable.

LOOKING AFTER YOUR WOK

Authentic Chinese woks made of carbon steel take some looking after, but if you care for your wok properly it will give you a lifetime of service. A carbon steel wok will never wear

DEEP-FRYING
Using a wok to deep-fry a selection of fish and vegetables.

out, no matter how often you use it, but it can become very rusty if not treated correctly.

If your wok has come from an oriental store it will probably be protected with a coating of oil when you buy it. This is easily removed with cream cleanser and hot water. Don't worry if you have to scrub really hard to remove it, as no amount of scrubbing can possibly damage the tough surface of carbon steel. After scrubbing and removing the oil, you will then need to 'season' your wok. To season a wok, place it over a low heat until it is dry and

hot, then remove it from the heat. Dip a wad of kitchen paper in a little vegetable oil, then rub this all over the inside of the wok until the paper becomes black. Discard the paper and start again with a clean wad and a little more oil, repeating this procedure as many times as it takes for the paper to stay clean and not turn black. Your wok will then be ready for use.

Every time you have finished using your wok, it must be washed in very hot water. For cleaning the wok, Chinese cooks use a special wok brush made from sticks of bamboo bound together at the handle end with more bamboo. This brush may look attractive and authentic, but it is by no means essential – an ordinary plastic kitchen brush will do the job just as well, plus a soapless scourer if necessary to detach any cooked pieces of food that have become stuck. After washing, the wok should be dried thoroughly and, before being put away, it must be wiped on the inside with a very thin film of oil using a wad of kitchen paper; this will prevent the carbon steel from going rusty during storage. If this happens despite the precautions taken, don't worry, simply scrub off the rust with a scourer and cream cleanser as you did when you first had your wok, then repeat the seasoning procedure.

STIR-FRYING IN A WOK

Stir-frying is the most common cooking method for which the wok is used. The wok's shape is perfectly designed for this technique, although steaming, braising and deep-frying are also possible.

The beauty of stir-frying lies in its speed and simplicity. The shape of

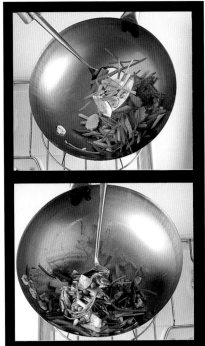

STIR-FRYING
Stir-frying a selection of thinly sliced vegetables and chicken.

the wok, together with the material it is made from and the way in which the food is prepared, all facilitate quick cooking.

The best fuel to use for stir-frying is gas, because it allows greater control of heat than electricity or solid fuel, and heat control is a very important part of the technique of stir-frying. The hob of a gas cooker also allows the wok to sit snugly and firmly immediately above the flame without wobbling about too much, but if you do not have gas, stir-frying is still possible with a flat-bottomed wok designed specifically for use on electric and solid fuel cookers.

Woks on stands are not very successful for stir-frying on a hob – the stand slows down the cooking and often the pan and oil simply do not get hot enough to cook the food quickly and successfully.

PREPARATION

For stir-frying to be successful, there are a few hints and tips that are worth knowing before you start. The correct preparation of ingredients, for example, is essential for the food to cook properly, and the techniques of slicing, cutting and chopping of meat, poultry, fish and vegetables are important ones.

Although it's unlikely that you will ever become quite as fast and dexterous as an oriental chef, there is no reason why these techniques should not become second nature to you with time and practice.

Ingredients used for stir-frying should always be very fresh and of the highest quality. This means using the best, lean and tender cuts of meat and poultry rather than the sinewy, tough cuts, and the freshest vegetables in season rather than those past their prime. The reason for this is that the food must cook in the shortest possible time – stir-frying makes the best of good food, but it cannot improve poor quality.

Always read through any stir-fry recipe from beginning to end before starting to prepare the ingredients and cook. Stir-frying allows no time for assembling and preparation once cooking has begun, so be sure to have all your ingredients to hand ready prepared and sliced before cooking. This includes the mixing together of any sauce ingredients, especially those with a cornflour thickening which should always be diluted in water and mixed to a paste before adding to the ingredients in the wok. Set everything out near the cooker, on a board for easy handling if you like. Although stir-frying involves quite a lot of advance preparation in this way, there is one consolation – once everything is prepared the majority of the hard work is over and the cooking can literally be done in minutes. This is a particular boon if you are entertaining, because you can easily prepare everything up to the cooking stage before your guests actually arrive.

CHOPPING AND SLICING TECHNIQUES

In the oriental kitchen, a cleaver is one of the most frequently-used pieces of equipment for preparing ingredients for stir-frying. Oriental cooks generally have several weights of cleaver for different purposes – slicing, cutting, shredding, mincing and chopping food, including bones – but this is not necessary for the average cook. Don't be put off buying a cleaver because you feel it looks dangerous. Cleavers are very easy to use, especially once you have had a little practice, but a very sharp, good-quality kitchen knife will do the job equally well.

With stir-frying, all ingredients are cooked very quickly, so there is very little time for food to absorb flavourings and seasonings. For this reason, and to speed up the cooking time, ingredients are cut thinly into pieces of uniform size and thickness, with as many cut surfaces as possible exposed. This is why vegetables are usually cut on the diagonal, or sometimes cut into 'julienne' strips, i.e. very fine 'squared-off' strips like matchsticks. Oriental chefs can cut vegetables into julienne strips with a cleaver at lightning speed, but you may find this technique time-consuming. It is well worth taking the time, however, because it makes the ingredients looks so attractive in the finished dish.

To cut vegetables such as carrots into julienne strips, top and tail them, then peel them and square off the sides. Cut crossways into 5 cm (2 inch) lengths, then slice each piece thinly lengthways. Stack the carrot slices on top of each other and slice lengthways again, cutting strips of even thickness.

Meat and poultry are usually cut thinly across the grain; this speeds up cooking and encourages maximum tenderness because most of the meat's surface is exposed to the heat. If you place the pieces of meat or poultry in the freezer to harden for about 1 hour before slicing, you will find this makes it far easier to cut the meat wafer thin, and by the time you have finished cutting it will be defrosted ready for cooking.

STARTING TO COOK IN THE WOK

Once you have prepared all your ingredients and they are assembled ready for cooking, you can start to stir-fry. Begin by preheating the wok for a few minutes over a low to moderate heat. This is essential because if you add oil and ingredients to a cold wok the chances are they will stick. Once the wok is hot, you can add the oil and heat this over a moderate heat until hot. This too is very important because the food must start cooking immediately it is added to the wok.

Most recipes start with the addition of ingredients such as onion or spring onions, fresh root ginger and garlic, because these are used to flavour the oil before the main ingredients are added. Take great care not to have the oil too hot at this stage and if necessary turn the heat down to low, as these flavouring ingredients have a tendency to burn. After the main ingredients have been added to the wok, you should immediately increase the heat to high so that the ingredients will cook in the shortest possible time.

Always add the ingredients to the wok in the order given in the recipe method. Stir-fry over a high heat unless otherwise stated, tossing and turning the ingredients all the time and moving them from the centre to the sides of the wok with a long-handled metal scoop or spatula. Shaped like a shovel with a wooden end, this is a useful piece of equipment for stir-frying as it is specially designed for tossing and turning the ingredients around the bottom and sides of the wok. An ordinary long-handled spoon or spatula can be used instead, but somehow these are not so effective. Chinese chefs often use long wooden 'cooking' chopsticks for stir-frying, but these can be tricky to work with unless you are used to them.

When pouring a sauce mixture into the wok towards the end of stir-frying, push the ingredients to one side of the wok and pour the sauce in at the other side. Toss the ingredients in the sauce over the highest possible heat so the sauce boils (and thickens if it contains cornflour).

DEEP-FRYING IN THE WOK

The Cantonese wok is ideal for deep-frying because of its round bottom and deep, sloping sides, and its two short handles on either side. Far less oil is needed than with a deep-fat fryer – to deep-fry enough ingredients for 4 people, for example, you will find that about 600 ml (1 pint) oil will be plenty. A vegetable oil such as groundnut is best for deep-frying because it has a high smoke point and a mild flavour, so it will not burn easily and neither will it taint the food. A metal wok stand is necessary for deep-frying, to provide a secure and stable base; this is essential if you are using a round-bottomed wok.

Another useful accessory for deep-frying is a rack for draining food that has been cooked; this clips on to the edge of the wok. Stands are either open-sided frames, or solid metal with holes around the sides.

For deep-frying there is no need to preheat the wok, simply pour in the oil and heat over a moderate heat to the desired temperature. If you have a deep-fat thermometer, you can get an accurate reading, but this is not essential as you can test the temperature of the oil by dropping in a small cube of stale bread and seeing how long it takes to turn golden brown all over. Both temperatures and timings are given in all deep-frying recipes in this book.

Never exceed the temperature recommended in a recipe or let the oil smoke because this can be very dangerous. Adding wet food to hot oil is also dangerous, so always make sure that the food is thoroughly dry before putting it into the hot oil. To take food in and out of the oil you will need a slotted spoon. Chinese spoons have long bamboo handles which are both attractive and helpful, but they are not essential. An ordinary slotted spoon is quite sufficient.

Never leave hot oil in the wok unattended. Even after you have finished cooking and turned off the heat, the oil will stay hot for a very long time.

STEAMING IN THE WOK

Steaming has always been a common cooking method in oriental countries, but nowadays it is becoming increasingly popular in the West because it is one of the healthiest ways to cook. With steaming, no fat is required and the natural flavour of the food can best be appreciated.

The easiest way to steam in a wok is with a special oriental-style bamboo steamer. This fits inside the wok on a wooden or metal trivet and comes complete with its own lid. Chinese bamboo steamers are very decorative, and have the advantage that they can be stacked on top of each other so that several foods can be cooked at the same time. Unless you plan to do a lot of steaming in the wok, a bamboo steamer is a luxury item, although it is attractive both to have on display in the kitchen and to carry to the table for serving.

If you do not have a special steamer, you can improvise by placing the food to be steamed on a plate which will fit inside the wok. Place a metal or wooden trivet in the bottom of the wok and put the wok on its stand on the hob. Pour in enough boiling water to just cover the trivet, then place the plate on the trivet and cover the wok with a lid. If your wok does not have its own lid, you can buy one separately in an oriental supermarket or hardware store – the high, dome-shaped variety is best. During steaming, be sure to check the water level from time to time and top up if necessary, to ensure that the water does not boil dry.

SPECIALIST INGREDIENTS

BAMBOO SHOOTS (2)

Available sliced and unsliced in cans from large supermarkets and oriental stores. Bamboo shoots themselves are bland in flavour, but they quickly absorb strong flavours such as soy sauce, ginger and garlic. They are the shoots from the base of the bamboo plant, picked when young and tender, parboiled, then canned in brine. They are a good storecupboard item, adding an instant oriental touch to stir-fries.

BEAN CURD (3)

This highly nutritious food is used extensively in the Far East; in Japan and Korea they call it 'tofu'. Made from soya beans, it is white in colour, with the texture of very soft cheese or junket. It is very high in protein, yet low in fat. Two basic types are available, the firm kind which you can buy in brine from oriental stores and some health food shops, and silken tofu, which is generally sold in long-life cartons in both supermarkets and health food shops. For stir-frying, the firm kind is best because it does not break up; silken tofu is good for sauces, soups and dips.

BEAN SAUCES (4, 17)

These are ready-made sauces sold in bottles in both supermarkets and oriental stores. They are excellent for imparting an instant authentic Chinese flavour to stir-fries, so are well worth keeping in your storecupboard (once opened they should be refrigerated). Black bean sauce is a classic Cantonese sauce, traditionally used with beef, but it can equally well be used with other meats and poultry, and with vegetables. It is made from salted black beans, onions, ginger and garlic, with oil, vinegar, sugar and seasoning. Yellow bean sauce is generally used with chicken as it is milder; it is made from salted soya beans, garlic, soy sauce, vinegar, sugar and seasoning.

BLACHAN (14) see Terasi

CHILLIES (18, 21)

Both fresh and dried chillies are widely available at supermarkets, greengrocers and Asian stores. The colour of fresh chillies can vary from green to bright red and mahogany brown, depending on the variety and degree of ripeness. The degree of 'hotness varies enormously,

and all chillies should therefore be treated with caution, although it is generally true to say that the smaller the chilli, the hotter it will be. Large, fat green chillies tend to be mild, for example, while the tiny thin green ones are usually fiery hot. Red chillies are simply the ripened form of green chillies, so tend to be sweeter and less sharp than their green counterparts. The seeds are the hottest part of any chilli and some – or all – of them can be included in a dish or not, according to personal taste. Wear rubber gloves to remove the seeds. Slit the chilli lengthways down the centre, then hold under the cold tap and gently rub off the seeds. If you ever handle chillies with bare hands, take great care to wash your hands well afterwards, and do not put your fingers near your eyes as the pungent juices of the chilli will irritate them and cause them to sting.

Chilli powder is made from ground dried red chillies, and is a convenient way to add hotness to food. Pure chilli powder is fiery hot and is generally used in small quantities, but some brands of chilli powder are not pure but are in fact blends of chilli powder, spices and

CHILLIES (continued)

seasonings, so check the label before you buy. Brands labelled 'chilli seasoning' are generally mild, a blend of chilli pepper, chilli seeds, cumin, salt, garlic and oregano. Chilli sauce is sold in bottles in oriental stores and supermarkets. It is a favourite sauce in the Far East, both for use in cooking and as a condiment. Made from hot chillies, vinegar, salt, tomato purée and spices, it is a good way to add spiciness and colour to a dish. Use with caution as brands vary – some are hot and sweet, others are sharp and vinegary.

CREAMED COCONUT (9)

This is sold in a hard block, usually weighing 200 g (7 oz), available from oriental stores and large supermarkets. It is used to make coconut milk, a rich, creamy liquid which forms the basis of many South-East Asian dishes, especially curries with thick sauces. All you have to do is chop it up and dissolve it in boiling water, then it can be added direct to the pan. Made commercially from fresh coconut, it is a much easier way to make coconut milk than by grating a fresh coconut yourself and letting it steep in boiling water, or by doing the same thing with desiccated coconut – both of which have to be strained before use (see page 45).

DAIKON (10)

Variously named 'Japanese white radish' and 'mooli', this curious-looking, long tapering root vegetable is bland in flavour, but has a good crisp texture. It can be found in many supermarkets as well as in Japanese and other oriental stores. It is inexpensive, so is well worth buying to add authenticity to stir-fries – it can be cut into julienne strips, grated or diced. The Japanese use it grated as a garnish; they also sculpt it into shapes.

FIVE-SPICE POWDER (15)

This is a blend of five different spices – cinnamon, cloves, star anise, fennel and

Szechuan pepper – used in Chinese cooking. It is aromatic rather than spicy, with a hint of liquorice flavour. Use it sparingly until you are used to its taste and aroma, but in any case it is always used in small quantities by the Chinese. You can grind and mix the various spices yourself if you like, but people tend to buy it ready ground.

GALINGAL (6, 7) see Lengkuas

GINGER (1)

Fresh ginger is a knobbly root, used extensively in oriental cooking, especially in stir-fries in conjunction with onions or spring onions, garlic and chillies. It is available from the fresh vegetable sections of supermarkets and oriental stores. Don't be put off by its odd appearance: its flavour is sweet and pungent – far superior to its dried counterpart, which should not be used as a substitute. To use fresh root ginger, peel off the skin, then chop or thinly slice the flesh, or pound it in a mortar and pestle or with the end of a rolling pin, or grate it, according to individual recipe instructions.

LAOS POWDER (25)

see Lengkuas

LEMON GRASS (13)

This is an aromatic herb which grows as a thin, tapering stem. It is widely used in the Far East, especially in Thailand, for its exquisite citrus flavour. The whole stem is bruised to help release its aroma and flavour and then it is added to curries and other dishes with sauce; it should be removed before serving. In stir-fries, the lower part of the stem is usually used, chopped finely or sliced thinly. 'Serai powder' is the name given to dried lemon grass and, as a rule of thumb, 1 teaspoon should be used per stem of the fresh herb. It is a poor substitute for fresh lemon grass, however, so try to use fresh when it is called for in a recipe. Fresh lemon grass

is available at some large supermarkets as well as in oriental stores and it keeps for several weeks if well wrapped and stored in the refrigerator. If you are unable to obtain lemon grass at all, you can use lemon or lime zest and juice instead, but the flavour will not be quite so lemony.

LENGKUAS (7)

A pine-flavoured root, sometimes also called galingal, used in the cuisines of South-East Asia. It looks similar to fresh root ginger, but is more resinous in flavour, with a mingled scent of pine and citrus. Peel and chop or slice it as you would root ginger. It is only available at oriental stores, so if you cannot obtain it, you can use the dried form instead. When ground this is known as 'laos powder'. Laos powder can be bought at some large supermarkets; while not so effective a flavouring as the fresh lengkuas, it is a good substitute.

MOOLI (10) see Daikon

NAM PLA (19)

This is the fish sauce that South-East Asians love to use – just as the Chinese seem addicted to soy sauce. Made from salted, fermented anchovies, it is a thin brown liquid which is added to stir-fries and used ubiquitously as a condiment. Despite its name, it is not particularly 'fishy' in flavour, but it does impart a unique saltiness that is one of the essential flavourings of this part of the world. Nam pla is only available at oriental stores, but it keeps indefinitely, so is well worth going out of your way for. If it is unobtainable, use bottled anchovy essence instead, or crushed canned anchovies.

OYSTER SAUCE (26)

A bottled Chinese sauce made from extract of oysters, salt and starch, this is the classic sauce for beef stir-fries. It is dark brown in colour and thick in consistency, and can be bought at most supermarkets as well as oriental stores.

RICE WINE (11)

Made from fermented rice, this is drunk by the Chinese with food, and used for cooking. It varies in colour from white to pale golden, depending on the brand – some are more expensive than others – and you will find a choice of different kinds in oriental supermarkets. For cooking, it is not necessary to buy the best kind. If you cannot get rice wine, you can use dry sherry instead, or a Japanese rice wine known as sake, which is similar to the Chinese version.

SERAI POWDER (13)

see Lemon Grass

SESAME OIL (22)

This highly aromatic oil with a distinctive nutty taste is derived from pressed, roasted sesame seeds, and its colour and flavour vary according to the length of time the seeds were roasted - the longer the roasting the darker the oil. It has a very low smoke point, so should not be used for stir-frying on its own. The best way to use it is to sprinkle it over the food in the wok just before serving – it has a very strong flavour, so you will only need 5-10 ml (1-2 teaspoons) at the most. It is widely available at supermarkets and health food shops as well as in oriental stores.

SESAME SEEDS (23)

These are used in oriental cooking not only to add flavour and texture, but also because they are extremely nutritious – they are high in protein, calcium and potassium as well as in B vitamins. If dry-fried in the wok for a minute or two, their nutty flavour is accentuated; they also become more brittle and easy to grind or crush. Both white and black sesame seeds are available, the white being the most common. The two colours taste the same, and are interchangeable in recipes.

SHIITAKE MUSHROOMS (24)

Fresh shiitake are now widely cultivated and sold in many large supermarkets as well as in oriental stores. They are very tasty mushrooms, with a firm texture; they do not shrink during cooking, so are well worth seeking out to use in oriental stir-fries. Dried shiitake mushrooms are sold at oriental stores in small packets. Their flavour is earthy and highly concentrated, so you only need to use them in very small quantities. Soak in warm water for 20 minutes before use: don't throw the soaking liquid away, but add it to the ingredients in the wok for extra flavour.

SOY SAUCE (12)

There are many different types of soy sauce, the best of which are made from naturally fermented soya beans, so check the label before you buy. (Japanese soy sauce, called shoyu, is always naturally fermented.) Light soy sauce is light in colour and thin in consistency, but salty in flavour, whereas dark soy sauce is dark, thick and sweet by comparison. The Chinese recommend light soy sauce for cooking, dark soy sauce for use in sauces and dips. The Indonesians have a very sweet soy sauce called kecap manis, but this is rarely available outside specialist shops.

SPRING ROLL WRAPPERS (8)

Made from flour and water, these paper-thin wrappers can only be bought in oriental stores, but they are well worth seeking out because they are shaped specifically for making Chinese spring rolls. If you are unable to obtain them, you can use ready-made filo pastry instead, but you will have to cut it into squares (as in the recipe for Spring Rolls on page 16).

SZECHUAN PEPPERCORNS (20)

These reddish-brown peppercorns are not related to ordinary pepper, and in fact look more like husks than peppercorns. They have a sharp, pungent aroma and flavour, which is released when the peppercorns are dry-fried, then crushed or ground. They are used extensively in the hot and spicy Szechuan cuisine of Western China. You can buy Szechuan peppercorns from the spice sections in most large supermarkets.

TERASI (14)

This is the Indonesian name for fermented salted shrimps or shrimp paste, sold in blocks and used as a flavouring throughout South-East Asia. The Malaysians call it blachan or balachan, the Burmese ngapi, and the Thais kapi, but they are all virtually the same. The paste is extremely pungent and salty, and is used in very small quantities. If it is not fried with spices, etc, at the beginning of a recipe, it should always be dry-fried, grilled or roasted before use. It is only available in oriental stores specialising in South-East Asian foods.

TOFU (3) see Bean Curd

WATER CHESTNUTS (5)

These are not chestnuts at all, but bulbs with a crisp white flesh and brown outer skin. They are available ready-peeled in cans from most large supermarkets. Although very bland in flavour, they are good for stir-fries because of their crisp texture.

WONTON SKINS (16)

These 7.5 cm (3 inch) square yellow wrappers are made from wheat flour, egg and water. They are sold in packets in Chinese supermarkets, and can be frozen for several months so they are worth buying and keeping in the freezer, if you are lucky enough to be able to get them. They are usually stuffed with minced meat or fish and then steamed or deep-fried, or poached and served in soup.

FISH & SHELLFISH

FISH AND SHELLFISH ARE TWO OF THE MOST POPULAR INGREDIENTS IN ORIENTAL COOKING. QUICK-COOKING AND LIGHT, THEY ARE BEST USED FRESH.

SINGAPORE CRAB

Ask the fishmonger to remove and discard the inedible parts of the crab for you, chop the body of the crab into serving pieces, and crack open the claws and legs.

2 TABLESPOONS VEGETABLE OIL

2.5 CM (1 INCH) PIECE FRESH ROOT GINGER, PEELED AND CHOPPED FINELY

1 CLOVE GARLIC, PEELED AND CHOPPED FINELY

1 TEASPOON HOT CHILLI POWDER

6 TABLESPOONS TOMATO KETCHUP

2 TABLESPOONS RED WINE VINEGAR

1 TABLESPOON SOFT BROWN SUGAR

150 ML (¼ PINT) BOILING FISH STOCK (SEE PAGE 29)

1 LARGE COOKED CRAB, CHOPPED INTO SERVING PIECES WITH CLAWS AND LEGS CRACKED OPEN

SALT

TO SERVE:

CUCUMBER CURLS OR SLICES

PRAWN CRACKERS

BOILED RICE

Heat the wok until hot. Add the oil and heat over a moderate heat until hot. Add the ginger and garlic and stir-fry for 2-3 minutes or until softened, taking care not to let them brown.

Add the chilli powder and stir well to combine, then add the ketchup, vinegar and sugar and stir until boiling. Add the boiling fish stock, then the pieces of crab. Stir-fry for about 5 minutes or until the crab is heated through, then add salt to taste. Serve hot, with cucumber curls, prawn crackers and boiled rice handed separately.

Serves 4 as a main dish, with accompaniments

SESAME PRAWNS

You will need raw prawns for this tasty starter. Splitting and pressing the prawns before cooking is not essential, but it does help prevent them shrivelling up during deep-frying.

12 RAW KING OR 'TIGER' PRAWNS

2 TABLESPOONS PLAIN FLOUR

1 LARGE EGG

2 TABLESPOONS SESAME SEEDS

SALT AND PEPPER

ABOUT 600 ML (1 PINT) VEGETABLE OIL FOR DEEP-FRYING

FLAT LEAF PARSLEY TO GARNISH

SOY SAUCE FOR DIPPING

Peel the prawns and remove the heads, keeping the tails on. Remove the black veins. Rinse the prawns under cold running water, then pat dry thoroughly. With a sharp pointed knife, slit the prawns along their undersides. Open the prawns out carefully, place cut side down on a board and press firmly on their backs to flatten them slightly.

Spread the flour out on a board or plate, add the prawns and turn to coat in the flour. Beat the egg in a bowl with the sesame seeds and salt and pepper to taste.

Pour the oil into the wok and heat to 180°C-190°C, 350°F-375°F, or until a cube of bread browns in 30 seconds.

Holding the prawns by their tails, dip them one at a time into the egg mixture, then immediately drop them into the hot oil. Deep-fry for 1-2 minutes or until crisp and light golden, then lift out with a slotted spoon and place on kitchen paper to drain. Keep hot while deep-frying the remaining prawns in the same way. Serve at once, garnished with flat leaf parsley, with a bowl of soy sauce for dipping.

Makes 12

MONKFISH WITH GARLIC AND SPRING ONIONS

Monkfish is one of the best fish for shallow-frying and stir-frying because its meaty, firm flesh does not break up during cooking. Although expensive, it has little waste, and its firm texture and superb flavour make it seem more substantial than other white fish. There is a generous amount of sauce with this stir-fry, so serve it spooned over plain steamed or boiled rice in Chinese bowls – the sauce will soak into the rice and make it tasty.

2 EGG WHITES

1 TABLESPOON CORNFLOUR

500 G (1 LB) MONKFISH TAILS, SKINNED AND CUT INTO BITE-SIZED PIECES

ABOUT 125 ML (4 FL OZ) VEGETABLE OIL FOR SHALLOW-FRYING

6 SPRING ONIONS, SLICED THINLY ON THE DIAGONAL

2 CLOVES GARLIC, CRUSHED

SALT AND PEPPER

SAUCE:

4 TABLESPOONS SOY SAUCE

2 TABLESPOONS RICE WINE OR DRY SHERRY

1 TABLESPOON RED WINE VINEGAR

2 TEASPOONS SOFT BROWN SUGAR

Lightly beat the egg whites and cornflour in a shallow dish with salt and pepper to taste. Add the monkfish and turn to coat, then set aside.

Mix the sauce ingredients together in a jug. Set aside.

Heat the wok until hot. Add the oil and heat over a moderate heat until hot but not smoking. With a fork, lift the monkfish out of the egg white mixture a piece at a time and lower into the hot oil. Shallow-fry in batches for 2-3 minutes or until golden on all sides. Lift out with a slotted spoon and place on kitchen paper to drain.

Pour off all but 1 tablespoon oil from the wok. Add the spring onions and garlic and stir-fry over a moderate heat for a few seconds. Pour in the sauce and bring to the boil, stirring, then return the monkfish to the wok. Toss until all the ingredients are combined and piping hot. Add pepper to taste and serve at once.

Serves 3-4 as a main dish with accompaniments, or as part of an oriental meal

SPRING ROLLS

You can use Chinese spring roll wrappers for these, but they are only available in oriental stores and frozen filo pastry is just as effective. Defrost the filo according to packet instructions, and keep it covered while using or it will dry out and crack.

4 FROZEN FILO SHEETS, DEFROSTED

BEATEN EGG FOR SEALING

ABOUT 600 ML (1 PINT) VEGETABLE OIL FOR DEEP-FRYING

FILLING:

1 TABLESPOON VEGETABLE OIL

1 RED PEPPER, CORED, SEEDED AND CHOPPED FINELY

4 SPRING ONIONS, CHOPPED FINELY

2.5 CM (1 INCH) PIECE FRESH ROOT GINGER, PEELED AND CHOPPED FINELY

175 G (6 OZ) BEAN SPROUTS

250 G (8 OZ) PEELED COOKED PRAWNS, DEFROSTED AND DRIED THOROUGHLY IF FROZEN, CHOPPED COARSELY

2 TEASPOONS SOY SAUCE

2 TEASPOONS RICE WINE OR DRY SHERRY

First make the filling: heat the wok until hot. Add the oil and heat over a moderate heat until hot. Add the red pepper, spring onions and ginger and stir-fry for 15 seconds. Add the bean sprouts and stir-fry for 1 minute or until just beginning to soften. Add the prawns, soy sauce and rice wine or sherry, increase the heat to high and stir-fry for a further 2 minutes, tossing the ingredients together until they are quite dry. Tip the mixture into a bowl and leave to cool. Wipe the inside of the wok clean with kitchen paper.

Cut each sheet of filo crossways in half to make 2 equal squares. Divide the filling into 8 equal portions. Place 1 filo square on the work surface and spoon 1 portion of the filling along the side nearest to you, about 4 cm (1½ inches) in from the edge. Bring this edge up, then roll it away from you a half turn over the filling. Fold the sides into the centre to enclose the filling, then brush all around the edges with a little beaten egg. Continue rolling the filo around the filling, then place join side downwards on a tray or board. Repeat with the remaining filo and filling.

Pour the oil for deep-frying into the wok and heat to 180°C-190°C, 350°F-375°F, or until a cube of bread browns in 30 seconds. Deep-fry half of the spring rolls for 4-5 minutes, or until the filo is golden brown and crisp. Lift out with a slotted spoon and drain on kitchen paper while deep-frying the remainder. Serve hot.

Makes 8

SPICY COCONUT PRAWNS

Chilli powder varies in strength from one brand to another, so take care to read the label before using. Pure chilli powder is fiery hot, and should be used with caution, while some chilli powders are mixtures of chilli and other spices and herbs. These mixtures are often labelled 'chilli seasoning' and are generally mild in flavour. Plain boiled rice is the best accompaniment for this rich, creamy dish, together with a cooling side salad of thinly sliced cucumber and chopped fresh mint.

100 G (3½ OZ) CREAMED COCONUT, CHOPPED ROUGHLY

2 TABLESPOONS VEGETABLE OIL

1 ONION, CHOPPED FINELY

1 CLOVE GARLIC, CRUSHED

500 G (1 LB) PEELED COOKED PRAWNS, DEFROSTED AND DRIED THOROUGHLY, IF FROZEN

2 TEASPOONS GROUND CORIANDER

1 TEASPOON GROUND CUMIN

1 TEASPOON TURMERIC

½ TEASPOON CHILLI POWDER

½ TEASPOON SALT, OR TO TASTE

SHREDDED FRESH COCONUT OR DESICCATED COCONUT FOR SPRINKLING (OPTIONAL)

First make the coconut milk: put the creamed coconut in a measuring jug, pour in boiling water up to the 300 ml (½ pint) mark and stir until the coconut is dissolved. Set aside.

Heat the wok until hot. Add the oil and heat over a moderate heat until hot. Add the onion and garlic and stir-fry for 1-2 minutes or until softened, taking care not to let them brown. Add the prawns and spices and stir-fry for a further 2 minutes. Remove the wok from the heat and tip the prawn mixture into a bowl. Set aside.

Pour the coconut milk slowly into the wok, stirring to scrape up any sediment from the sides and bottom. Return the wok to a high heat and bring the coconut milk to the boil, stirring constantly. Lower the heat and simmer for 5 minutes or until the coconut milk thickens, stirring constantly.

Return the prawn mixture to the wok and toss for 1-2 minutes or until piping hot. Add salt to taste. Serve hot, sprinkled with shredded fresh coconut or desiccated coconut, if you like.

Serves 4 as a main dish, with accompaniments

STEAMED WHOLE FISH

In this recipe two small sea bass fit neatly into a bamboo steamer, which in turn fits inside the wok. If only large sea bass is available, you can steam it in a fish kettle, or on a rack in a large roasting pan.

2 x 500 G (1 LB) SEA BASS, GUTTED, WITH HEADS AND TAILS LEFT ON

2 LARGE BUNCHES SPRING ONIONS, SHREDDED FINELY

2 CELERY STICKS, CUT INTO JULIENNE STRIPS

5 CM (2 INCH) PIECE FRESH ROOT GINGER, PEELED AND CUT INTO JULIENNE STRIPS

ABOUT 4 TABLESPOONS VEGETABLE OIL

4 TABLESPOONS SOY SAUCE

6 TABLESPOONS RICE WINE OR DRY SHERRY

1 TABLESPOON SESAME OIL

1 TEASPOON CASTER SUGAR

PEPPER

Wash the fish inside and out, then dry thoroughly. With scissors, cut the tails into 'V' shapes. With a sharp knife, make several deep diagonal slashes on both sides of each fish.

Place the fish on a plate that will fit inside a bamboo steamer. Place a quarter of the spring onions inside the fish, together with half of the celery and ginger. Brush the outside of the fish lightly with about 2 tablespoons oil. Sprinkle another quarter of the spring onions over the fish, with the remaining celery and ginger, then half of the soy sauce and the rice wine or sherry.

Cover the steamer with its lid, then place in the wok on a trivet. Carefully pour water down the side of the steamer until the base of the steamer is immersed in water, then place the wok on its stand over a high heat. Bring the water to the boil, then simmer for 15 minutes or until the flesh of the fish is opaque when tested near the bone. Check the water level occasionally and add more if necessary.

Heat 2 tablespoons vegetable oil and the sesame oil in a heavy frying pan, add the remaining soy sauce and the sugar and stir well to mix. Add the remaining spring onions and pepper to taste and stir to combine.

Remove and discard the flavourings from the top of the fish. Transfer the fish to a warmed large serving plate, arranging them head-to-toe fashion. Arrange the pieces of freshly cooked spring onion over the fish in a criss-cross pattern and drizzle with the cooking liquid. Serve at once.

Serves 4 as a main dish, with accompaniments

WARM THAI SALAD

6 TABLESPOONS VEGETABLE OIL

1 BUNCH SPRING ONIONS, SLICED THINLY ON THE DIAGONAL

5 CM (2 INCH) PIECE FRESH ROOT GINGER, PEELED AND CHOPPED FINELY

1 SKINNED AND BONED CHICKEN BREAST, CUT INTO THIN STRIPS ON THE DIAGONAL

2 TABLESPOONS NAM PLA (FISH SAUCE)

500 G (1 LB) PEELED COOKED PRAWNS, DEFROSTED AND DRIED THOROUGHLY, IF FROZEN

FLAT LEAF PARSLEY TO GARNISH

HOT DRESSING:

2 FRESH RED OR GREEN CHILLIES, SEEDED AND CHOPPED ROUGHLY

2 LARGE CLOVES GARLIC, CHOPPED ROUGHLY

GRATED RIND OF 1 LIME OR LEMON

JUICE OF 3 LIMES OR LEMONS

2 TABLESPOONS NAM PLA (FISH SAUCE)

1 TABLESPOON SOFT BROWN SUGAR

SALAD:

½ HEAD CRISP LETTUCE, SHREDDED

1 BUNCH RADISHES, SLICED THINLY

½ CUCUMBER, SLICED THINLY

First prepare the hot dressing: pound the chillies in a mortar and pestle with the garlic and grated lime or lemon rind to make a rough kind of paste. Stir in the lime or lemon juice, nam pla and sugar. Set aside.

Mix all the salad ingredients together in a bowl. Set aside. Heat the wok until hot. Add 2 tablespoons of the oil and heat over a moderate heat until hot. Add half of the spring onions and ginger and stir-fry for a few seconds to flavour the oil, then add the chicken and sprinkle over half of the nam pla. Increase the heat to high and stir-fry for 3-4 minutes or until the chicken is lightly coloured on all sides. Remove the wok from the heat and transfer the chicken to a plate with a slotted spoon. Keep hot. Stir-fry the prawns in the same way as the chicken, using more oil, the remaining spring onions, ginger and nam pla. Keep hot.

Heat the remaining oil in the wok over a moderate heat, pour in the dressing and stir until hot. Add the chicken and prawns and their juices and toss to mix with the dressing. Pour the contents of the wok over the salad ingredients, toss to combine and serve at once, garnished with flat leaf parsley.

Serves 3-4 as a main dish

LOBSTER AND MANGO HOT SALAD

This subtly flavoured 'salad' is simple and quick, though expensive. It is the ideal dish for a lunch or dinner party at short notice when time is limited and money no object! Cooked whole lobsters can be bought at the fresh fish counters of large supermarkets and at good fishmongers. Ask the fishmonger to get the lobster ready for you so that all you have to do is remove the meat from the shell – he may even do this for you if you give him some notice.

2 RIPE MANGOES, PEELED AND SLICED

3 TABLESPOONS VEGETABLE OIL

1 BUNCH SPRING ONIONS, SLICED THINLY ON THE DIAGONAL

2 TEASPOONS GROUND CORIANDER

15 G (½ OZ) BUTTER

MEAT FROM 1 LARGE LOBSTER, CUT INTO BITE-SIZED PIECES

2 TABLESPOONS DRY SHERRY

2 TABLESPOONS DRY WHITE WINE

150 ML (¼ PINT) DOUBLE CREAM

2 TABLESPOONS FINELY CHOPPED CORIANDER

SALT AND PEPPER

TO GARNISH:

MIXED SALAD

FRESH CORIANDER LEAVES

Fan the mango slices out attractively on 4 dinner plates; cover and set aside.

Heat the wok until hot. Add 2 tablespoons of the oil and heat over a moderate heat until hot. Add the spring onions and ground coriander and stir-fry for a few seconds or until the onions are softened slightly but not limp. Remove the wok from the heat and transfer the spring onions to kitchen paper with a slotted spoon. Leave to drain.

Return the wok to a moderate heat. Add the butter with the remaining oil and heat until foaming, then add the lobster and toss to coat. Add the sherry and wine, with salt and pepper to taste, and toss the ingredients together for 1-2 minutes.

Add the cream and toss to coat, then return the spring onions to the wok and add the chopped coriander. Heat through gently, shaking the wok constantly, then taste for seasoning and adjust if necessary.

Arrange the pieces of lobster next to the mango slices and garnish with salad and coriander leaves. Serve at once.

Serves 4 as a main dish

MIXED FISH TEMPURA

8 RAW KING OR 'TIGER' PRAWNS

375 G (12 OZ) MONKFISH TAILS

175 G (6 OZ) PREPARED SQUID, QUILLS REMOVED

A LITTLE PLAIN FLOUR FOR DUSTING

ABOUT 600 ML (1 PINT) VEGETABLE OIL FOR DEEP-FRYING

LEMON WEDGES TO SERVE

BATTER:

125 G (4 OZ) PLAIN FLOUR

2 TABLESPOONS ARROWROOT

2 TABLESPOONS MAIZE FLOUR

PINCH OF SALT

300 ML (½ PINT) ICED WATER

HOT DIPPING SAUCE:

4 TABLESPOONS SOY SAUCE

4 TABLESPOONS RICE WINE OR DRY SHERRY

1 TABLESPOON FINELY CHOPPED ROOT GINGER

1 TEASPOON GRATED HORSERADISH OR PREPARED MUSTARD

½ TEASPOON CLEAR HONEY

First make the batter: sift the plain flour, arrowroot and maize flour into a bowl with the salt. Add the water a little at a time, whisking constantly. Cover and chill for 30 minutes.

Meanwhile, prepare the fish: peel the prawns and remove the heads, keeping the tails on. Remove the black veins. Rinse the prawns under cold water, then dry thoroughly. With a sharp knife, slit prawns along their undersides. Open out carefully, place cut side down on a board and press down firmly on their backs to flatten slightly. Skin the monkfish and cut into bite-sized pieces. Slice the bodies of the squid into 1 cm (½ inch) wide rings. Leave the tentacles whole or chop, depending on size. Blanch in boiling water for 30 seconds, drain, then rinse under cold water and pat dry. Dust all the fish lightly with flour.

Make the hot dipping sauce: put all the ingredients in a small bowl and whisk until the honey is dissolved.

Heat the oil in the wok to 180°C-190°C, 350°F-375°F. Holding the prawns by their tails, dip them one at a time into the batter, then drop them into the hot oil. Deep-fry for 2-3 minutes or until crisp and golden, then lift out with a slotted spoon and drain on kitchen paper. Keep hot. Deep-fry the monkfish and squid in batches in the same way, using a fork to dip each piece into the batter and then dropping it into the hot oil. Serve as soon as all the fish are cooked, with the dipping sauce and lemon wedges handed separately.

Serves 4 as a starter or light main course

SESAME PRAWN TOASTS

Fingers of bread are topped with a tasty prawn and spring onion mixture, then sprinkled with sesame seeds and deep-fried. Crisp and crunchy, they make an interesting starter before a Chinese meal, served with soy sauce for dipping. If you are worried about deep-frying when guests arrive, you can make the prawn toasts up to an hour beforehand and keep them hot in a moderate oven.

250 G (8 OZ) PEELED COOKED PRAWNS, DEFROSTED AND

DRIED THOROUGHLY, IF FROZEN

2 SPRING ONIONS, CHOPPED ROUGHLY

2 CLOVES GARLIC, CHOPPED ROUGHLY

2 TABLESPOONS CORNFLOUR

2 TEASPOONS SOY SAUCE

12 SLICES STALE WHITE BREAD (FROM A LARGE THICK

SLICED LOAF), CRUSTS REMOVED

65 G (2½ OZ) SESAME SEEDS

ABOUT 600 ML (1 PINT) VEGETABLE OIL, FOR DEEP-FRYING

SPRING ONION TASSELS (SEE PAGE 73) TO GARNISH

SOY SAUCE FOR DIPPING

Work the prawns to a paste in a food processor with the spring onions, garlic, cornflour and soy sauce.

Cut each slice of bread into 3 fingers. Spread the prawn paste thickly on one side of each finger of bread, then sprinkle evenly with sesame seeds. Press the seeds down firmly, then chill the fingers in the refrigerator for about 30 minutes, to firm them up.

Pour the oil into the wok and heat to 180°C-190°C, 350°F-375°F, or until a cube of bread browns in 30 seconds. Deep-fry the toasts a few at a time, paste side down, for 2-3 minutes or until golden. Lift out with a slotted spoon and drain, paste side up, on kitchen paper. Serve hot, garnished with spring onion tassels. Hand soy sauce for dipping in a small bowl.

Makes 36

CRAB CURRY WITH COCONUT

Stems of fresh lemon grass can be bought in oriental stores and some large supermarkets. They are used in South-East Asian cooking for their strong, aromatic citrus flavour. In this recipe, the whole stem is bruised to help release the flavour into the coconut sauce, and the stem is then removed before serving.

100 G (3½ OZ) CREAMED COCONUT, CHOPPED ROUGHLY

3 TABLESPOONS VEGETABLE OIL

1 SMALL ONION, CHOPPED FINELY

5 CM (2 INCH) PIECE FRESH ROOT GINGER, PEELED AND CHOPPED FINELY

4 CLOVES GARLIC, CRUSHED

2 TEASPOONS CHILLI POWDER, OR TO TASTE

2 TEASPOONS GROUND CORIANDER

1 TEASPOON TURMERIC

DARK AND WHITE MEAT FROM 1 LARGE DRESSED CRAB

1 STEM LEMON GRASS, BRUISED, OR THINLY PARED RIND OF 1 LEMON

½ TEASPOON SALT

TO GARNISH:

CHOPPED FRESH CORIANDER LEAVES

DESICCATED COCONUT

First make the coconut milk: put the chopped coconut in a measuring jug, pour in boiling water up to the 300 ml (½ pint) mark and stir until the coconut is dissolved. Set aside.

Heat the wok until hot. Add the oil and heat over a moderate heat until hot. Add the onion, ginger and garlic and stir-fry for 2-3 minutes or until softened, taking care not to let the ingredients brown. Add the chilli powder, coriander and turmeric and stir-fry for 1-2 minutes longer.

Add the dark crab meat, the coconut milk, lemon grass or lemon rind and the salt. Bring slowly to the boil, stirring, then simmer for about 15 minutes or until thickened, stirring frequently.

Turn the heat down to very low. Remove the lemon grass or lemon rind and discard. Add the white crab meat to the coconut sauce and heat through very gently, shaking the wok occasionally and taking care not to break up the pieces of crab or let the sauce catch on the bottom of the wok. Serve at once, sprinkled with coriander and coconut.

Serves 2-3 as a main dish with accompaniments, 4 as part of an oriental meal

BRAISED GREY MULLET WITH BLACK BEAN SAUCE

Grey mullet is highly prized by Chinese cooks for its delicate flavour and texture. Served with an oriental-style black bean sauce as in this recipe, it makes a delicious meal for 2 people. Accompany the fish with bowls of plain boiled rice, with some of the sauce spooned over. Ready-prepared black bean sauce is available in jars in the Chinese food sections of most supermarkets, as well as in oriental stores.

1 x 500-750 G (1-1½ LB) GREY MULLET, GUTTED, WITH HEAD AND TAIL LEFT ON

1 TABLESPOON CORNFLOUR

ABOUT 600 ML (1 PINT) VEGETABLE OIL FOR DEEP-FRYING

3 SPRING ONIONS, SLICED THINLY ON THE DIAGONAL

2.5 CM (1 INCH) PIECE FRESH ROOT GINGER, PEELED AND CUT INTO JULIENNE STRIPS

1 CLOVE GARLIC, CRUSHED

125 ML (4 FL OZ) FISH STOCK (SEE PAGE 29) OR FISH STOCK MADE FROM A CUBE

2 TABLESPOONS BLACK BEAN SAUCE

2 TABLESPOONS SOY SAUCE

2 TABLESPOONS RICE WINE OR DRY SHERRY

SHREDDED SPRING ONIONS TO GARNISH

Wash the fish inside and out, then dry thoroughly. With kitchen shears or scissors, cut the tail into a 'V' shape. With a sharp knife, make several deep diagonal slashes on both sides of the fish. Dust the fish with the cornflour.

Pour the oil into the wok and heat to 180°C-190°C, 350°F-375°F, or until a cube of bread browns in 30 seconds. Using a fish slice, carefully lower the fish into the hot oil and deep-fry for 1-2 minutes on each side. Remove the wok from the heat and transfer the fish to kitchen paper, using a fish slice. Leave the fish to drain on the paper.

Pour off all but 2 tablespoons oil from the wok. Return the wok to a moderate heat, add the spring onions, ginger and garlic and stir-fry for 2-3 minutes or until softened, taking care not to let the ingredients brown.

Stir in the stock, black bean and soy sauces and the rice wine or sherry. Bring to the boil, stirring, then return the fish to the wok. Lower the heat, cover the wok and braise the fish for 5 minutes on each side, turning once and basting frequently with the sauce. Serve at once, garnished with shredded spring onions.

Serves 2 as a main dish, with accompaniments

RAPID-FRIED CHILLI PRAWNS WITH CHERRY TOMATOES

Raw 'tiger' prawn tails are available at good fishmongers and the fresh fish counters of large supermarkets. They are expensive, but they are also large, juicy, and full of flavour – far superior to the ubiquitous pale pink cooked variety. Serve this dish as part of an oriental meal, with noodles or rice. Chillies vary in 'hotness' according to their variety, but whatever type they are it is the seeds that are the hottest part, so include as few – or as many – as you dare!

3 TABLESPOONS VEGETABLE OIL

1 SMALL ONION, CHOPPED FINELY

2.5 CM (1 INCH) PIECE FRESH ROOT GINGER, PEELED AND CHOPPED FINELY

2 CLOVES GARLIC, CRUSHED

1-2 FRESH CHILLIES OR 1-2 TEASPOONS CHILLI POWDER, ACCORDING TO TASTE

350 G (12 OZ) RAW 'TIGER' PRAWN TAILS, DEFROSTED AND DRIED THOROUGHLY, IF FROZEN, PEELED

6-8 CHERRY TOMATOES, HALVED

2 TABLESPOONS TOMATO PURÉE

1 TABLESPOON WINE VINEGAR (RED OR WHITE)

PINCH OF CASTER SUGAR

½ TEASPOON SALT

CORIANDER SPRIGS TO GARNISH

Heat the wok until hot. Add the oil and heat over a moderate heat until hot. Add the onion, ginger, garlic and chillies or chilli powder and stir-fry for 2-3 minutes or until softened, taking care not to let the ingredients brown.

Add the prawns, increase the heat to high and stir-fry for 1-2 minutes or until they turn pink. Add the tomatoes, tomato purée, wine vinegar, sugar and salt. Increase the heat to high and stir-fry for several minutes or until the mixture is thick, taking care not to let the cherry tomatoes lose their shape. Taste and add more salt if necessary. Serve at once, garnished with sprigs of coriander.

Serves 4 as part of an oriental meal

DEEP-FRIED WONTONS

Deep golden yellow wonton skins are available in Chinese supermarkets. This method of folding them to make 'pouches' is very simple and ensures that the filling stays safely inside the skins during deep-frying.

24 WONTON SKINS, EACH ABOUT 8 CM (3½ INCHES) SQUARE

ABOUT 600 ML (1 PINT) VEGETABLE OIL FOR DEEP-FRYING

FILLING:

175 G (6 OZ) PEELED COOKED PRAWNS, DEFROSTED AND DRIED THOROUGHLY, IF FROZEN

2 SPRING ONIONS, CHOPPED ROUGHLY

2.5 CM (1 INCH) PIECE FRESH ROOT GINGER, PEELED AND CHOPPED ROUGHLY

1 CLOVE GARLIC, CHOPPED ROUGHLY

1 EGG YOLK

1 TABLESPOON SOY SAUCE

1 TEASPOON CASTER SUGAR

PEPPER

DIPPING SAUCE:

1 FRESH CHILLI, SEEDED AND CHOPPED VERY FINELY

3 TABLESPOONS SOY SAUCE

1 TABLESPOON WINE VINEGAR (RED OR WHITE)

1 TABLESPOON SESAME OIL

2 TEASPOONS CASTER SUGAR

First make the filling: work the prawns, spring onions, ginger and garlic in a food processor or mincer until finely minced. Add the egg yolk, soy sauce, sugar and pepper to taste and work again until evenly mixed.

Using a teaspoon, place a little of the filling mixture in the centre of each wonton skin, brush the edges with a little water, then bring up 2 opposite corners of the skins over the filling to form triangular shapes. Bring the 2 bottom corners of each triangle to meet in the centre and slightly overlap them to make an envelope shape. Press all the edges firmly to seal.

Make the dipping sauce: put all the ingredients in a small bowl and whisk until the sugar is dissolved.

Pour the oil into the wok and heat to 180°C-190°C, 350°F-375°F, or until a cube of bread browns in 30 seconds. Deep-fry 4-6 wontons at a time in the hot oil for 2-3 minutes, or until puffed up, golden and crisp. Lift out with a slotted spoon and drain on kitchen paper. Keep hot while deep-frying the remaining wontons in the same way. Serve the wontons hot, with the dipping sauce handed separately.

Makes 24

SWEET GARLIC PRAWNS

This simple recipe has very few ingredients, so it is quick to assemble and cook. Remember that the prawns are already cooked and only need to be heated through. Do not overcook them or they will shrink and become tough and rubbery.

2 TABLESPOONS VEGETABLE OIL

4 CLOVES GARLIC, CRUSHED

2.5 CM (1 INCH) PIECE FRESH ROOT GINGER, PEELED AND

CUT INTO JULIENNE STRIPS

1-2 TEASPOONS CHILLI POWDER, ACCORDING TO TASTE

500 G (1 LB) PEELED COOKED PRAWNS, DEFROSTED AND

DRIED THOROUGHLY, IF FROZEN

SAUCE:

2 TEASPOONS CORNFLOUR

4 TABLESPOONS COLD FISH STOCK (SEE PAGE 29) OR

FISH STOCK MADE FROM A CUBE

4 TABLESPOONS SOY SAUCE

2 TABLESPOONS CLEAR HONEY

First prepare the sauce: mix the cornflour to a paste with a little of the fish stock, then stir in the remaining fish stock, the soy sauce and honey. Set aside.

Heat the wok until hot. Add the oil and heat over a moderate heat until hot. Add the garlic, ginger and chilli powder and stir-fry for 2-3 minutes or until softened, taking care not to let the ingredients brown. Add the prawns and stir-fry for 1-2 minutes, just until they are hot.

Stir the sauce to mix, then pour over the prawns. Increase the heat to high and toss just until the prawns are coated in the sauce. Serve at once.

Serves 3-4 as a main dish with accompaniments, or as part of an oriental meal

FISH FILLETS IN HOT SAUCE

Because of its delicate texture, white fish has a tendency to break up during stir-frying. This method of coating strips of fish in egg white and cornflour and then deep-frying them in hot oil is good for holding the pieces of fish together. The batter is light and delicate, and the hot sauce provides a good sharp contrast of flavours. If you prefer not to deep-fry the fish, then it is best to use a firm-fleshed fish such as monkfish, in which case it need not be coated in batter and can simply be stir-fried in a few tablespoons of hot oil.

1 EGG WHITE

500 G (1 LB) WHITE FISH FILLETS, PREFERABLY PLAICE, CUT

INTO CHUNKY STRIPS

2 TABLESPOONS CORNFLOUR

ABOUT 600 ML (1 PINT) VEGETABLE OIL FOR DEEP-FRYING

STEAMED OR BOILED RICE TO SERVE

SAUCE:

150 ML (¼ PINT) FISH STOCK (SEE PAGE 29) OR

FISH STOCK MADE FROM A CUBE

2 TABLESPOONS SOY SAUCE

2 TABLESPOONS CHILLI SAUCE

1 TABLESPOON LEMON JUICE

1 TABLESPOON TOMATO PURÉE

2 TEASPOONS SOFT BROWN SUGAR

Lightly beat the egg white in a shallow dish, add the strips of fish and turn to coat. Spread the cornflour out on a board or plate, then dip the fish in the cornflour until lightly coated on all sides.

Pour the oil into the wok and heat to 180°C-190°C, 350°F-375°F, or until a cube of bread browns in 30 seconds. Drop a few pieces of fish into the hot oil, then deep-fry for 1-2 minutes or until golden. Lift out with a slotted spoon, drain on kitchen paper and keep hot. Repeat with the remaining strips of fish.

Pour off all the oil from the wok and wipe the inside clean with kitchen paper. Add all the sauce ingredients to the wok, return to a moderate heat and bring to the boil, stirring. Simmer until the sauce is reduced slightly, then lower the heat, return the fish to the wok and heat through for 1 minute. Serve at once, over individual bowls of steamed or boiled rice.

Serves 3-4 as a main dish, with rice as an accompaniment

SZECHUAN SQUID

Ready-prepared squid is available at the fresh fish counters of large supermarkets. It is very convenient to buy it in this way as whole fresh squid with their ink sacs intact are time-consuming and messy to deal with. Choose the smallest squid available, as these will be the most tender, but in any case never overcook squid or it will be tough and chewy.

500 G (1 LB) PREPARED SQUID, QUILLS REMOVED

3 TABLESPOONS VEGETABLE OIL

1 MEDIUM ONION, SLICED THINLY INTO RINGS

1 RED PEPPER, CORED, SEEDED AND SLICED THINLY INTO RINGS

1 YELLOW OR GREEN PEPPER, CORED, SEEDED AND SLICED THINLY INTO RINGS

1 FRESH CHILLI, SEEDED AND SLICED THINLY INTO RINGS

SAUCE:

1 TABLESPOON CORNFLOUR

4 TABLESPOONS WATER

2 CLOVES GARLIC, CRUSHED

3 TABLESPOONS SOY SAUCE

2 TABLESPOONS CHILLI SAUCE

1 TEASPOON CASTER SUGAR

Slice the bodies of the squid neatly into 1 cm (½ inch) thick rings. Leave the tentacles whole or chop them, depending on their size. Blanch the squid in boiling water for 30 seconds, drain, then rinse under cold water and pat dry. Set aside.

Prepare the sauce: mix the cornflour to a thin paste with the water, then stir in the garlic, soy and chilli sauces and sugar. Set aside.

Heat the wok until hot. Add 2 tablespoons of the oil and heat over a moderate heat until hot. Add the onion, peppers and chilli and stir-fry for 5 minutes or until the peppers are tender. Remove the wok from the heat and transfer the pepper mixture to a plate with a slotted spoon. Set aside.

Return the wok to a moderate heat. Add the remaining oil and heat until hot. Add the squid rings and tentacles and stir-fry for 2-3 minutes or until just tender. Remove with a slotted spoon and set aside with the vegetables.

Stir the sauce to mix, then pour into the wok. Increase the heat to high and stir vigorously until boiling, then return the squid and vegetables and their juices to the wok and toss until coated in the sauce and piping hot. Serve at once.

Serves 3-4 as a main dish with accompaniments, or as part of an oriental meal

SCALLOPS WITH LEMON AND GINGER

8 SHELLED SCALLOPS WITH CORAL, DEFROSTED AND DRIED THOROUGHLY, IF FROZEN

15 G (½ OZ) BUTTER

2 TABLESPOONS VEGETABLE OIL

½ BUNCH SPRING ONIONS, SLICED THINLY ON THE DIAGONAL

½ TEASPOON TURMERIC

3 TABLESPOONS LEMON JUICE

2 TABLESPOONS RICE WINE OR DRY SHERRY

2 PIECES STEM GINGER, WITH SYRUP, CHOPPED

SALT AND PEPPER

LEMON SLICES OR SEGMENTS TO GARNISH

Slice the scallops thickly, detaching the corals and keeping them whole. Set the corals aside.

Heat the wok until hot. Add the butter and 1 tablespoon of the oil and heat over a gentle heat until foaming. Add the sliced scallops and stir-fry for 3 minutes. Remove the wok from the heat and transfer the scallops to a plate with a slotted spoon. Set aside.

Return the wok to a moderate heat, add the remaining oil and heat until hot. Add the spring onions and turmeric and stir-fry for a few seconds. Add the lemon juice and rice wine or sherry and bring to the boil, then stir in the stem ginger.

Return the scallops and their juices to the wok and toss until heated through. Add the reserved coral and stir-fry for a further minute. Add salt and pepper to taste and serve at once, garnished with lemon.

Serves 2 as a main dish, with accompaniments

SWEET AND SOUR SWORDFISH

Swordfish fillets are available at fish counters in many large supermarkets. They are ideal for stir-frying as their texture is firm and meaty and they do not fall apart – unlike other white fish such as plaice, haddock and cod. Plain noodles or boiled rice would be the best accompaniment.

500 G (1 LB) SWORDFISH FILLETS, CUT INTO CHUNKY STRIPS

3 TABLESPOONS VEGETABLE OIL

1 TABLESPOON CORNFLOUR

125 ML (4 FL OZ) COLD FISH STOCK (SEE PAGE 29) OR FISH STOCK MADE FROM A CUBE

1 GREEN PEPPER, CORED, SEEDED AND CUT LENGTHWAYS INTO THIN STRIPS

1 RED PEPPER, CORED, SEEDED AND CUT LENGTHWAYS INTO THIN STRIPS

MARINADE:

3 TABLESPOONS SOY SAUCE

2 TABLESPOONS RICE WINE OR DRY SHERRY

1 TABLESPOON WINE VINEGAR (RED OR WHITE)

1 TABLESPOON SOFT BROWN SUGAR

First make the marinade: put the soy sauce and rice wine or sherry in a shallow dish with the wine vinegar and sugar. Add the swordfish and turn gently to coat. Cover and leave to marinate for about 30 minutes, turning the fish occasionally.

Heat the wok until hot. Add 2 tablespoons of the oil and heat over a moderate heat until hot. Lift the strips of swordfish out of the marinade with a slotted spoon, draining off as much of the liquid as possible. Reserve the marinating liquid in the dish. Add the swordfish to the wok and stir-fry for 3-5 minutes, or until tender. Remove the wok from the heat and transfer the swordfish to a plate with a slotted spoon. Set aside.

Mix the cornflour to a paste with a little of the fish stock, then stir in the reserved marinating liquid and the remaining fish stock. Set aside.

Return the wok to a moderate heat. Add the remaining oil and heat until hot. Add the pepper strips and stir-fry for 5 minutes. Stir the cornflour and fish stock to mix, then pour into the wok and bring to the boil, stirring constantly. Return the swordfish and its juices to the wok, increase the heat to high and toss for 1-2 minutes or until all the ingredients are combined and piping hot. Serve at once with boiled rice.

Serves 4 as a main dish, with accompaniments

SAUTÉ OF SCALLOPS WITH MANGETOUT

Frozen shelled scallops are available at most good fishmongers, and at the fresh fish counters of many large supermarkets. They are expensive, but quite rich in flavour, so you do not need a large quantity. This recipe allows 4 scallops per person, but you could increase this to 5-6 if you feel 4 is not enough. The orange coral looks so pretty nestling amongst the green mangetout that you might want to increase the orange colour, in which case you could cut some thin carrot slices into half moon shapes, blanch them, then add them to the wok with the mangetout – these would be a similar shape to the coral but infinitely cheaper.

8 SHELLED SCALLOPS WITH CORAL, DEFROSTED AND DRIED THOROUGHLY, IF FROZEN

3 TABLESPOONS VEGETABLE OIL

6 SPRING ONIONS, SLICED THINLY ON THE DIAGONAL

2.5 CM (1 INCH) PIECE FRESH ROOT GINGER, PEELED AND CHOPPED FINELY

175 G (6 OZ) MANGETOUT, TOPS REMOVED

1 CLOVE GARLIC, CRUSHED

1 TABLESPOON SESAME OIL

2 TABLESPOONS SOY SAUCE

½ TEASPOON CASTER SUGAR

PEPPER

SPRING ONIONS TO GARNISH

Slice the scallops thickly, detaching the corals and keeping them whole. Set the corals aside.

Heat the wok until hot. Add 2 tablespoons of the vegetable oil and heat over a moderate heat until hot. Add the spring onions and ginger and stir-fry for a few seconds. Add the mangetout and garlic and stir-fry for 2 minutes more, then remove the wok from the heat and tip the contents into a bowl. Set aside.

Return the wok to a moderate heat. Add the remaining vegetable oil and the sesame oil and sliced scallops and stir-fry for 3 minutes. Return the spring onion, ginger and mangetout mixture to the wok, add the reserved corals, soy sauce and sugar and increase the heat to high. Toss for 1-2 minutes or until all the ingredients are combined and piping hot. Add pepper to taste and then serve at once, garnished with spring onions.

Serves 2 as a main dish, with accompaniments

FIVE-SPICE FISH

500 G (1 LB) MONKFISH TAILS, SKINNED AND CUT INTO

CHUNKY PIECES

2 EGG WHITES

4 TEASPOONS CORNFLOUR

ABOUT 300 ML (½ PINT) VEGETABLE OIL FOR

SHALLOW-FRYING

125 ML (4 FL OZ) WATER

SPRING ONION TASSELS (SEE PAGE 73) TO

GARNISH (OPTIONAL)

MARINADE:

2.5 CM (1 INCH) PIECE FRESH ROOT GINGER,

CHOPPED FINELY

3 TABLESPOONS SOY SAUCE

3 TABLESPOONS RICE WINE OR DRY SHERRY

2 TEASPOONS DARK SOFT BROWN SUGAR

1 TEASPOON FIVE-SPICE POWDER

First make the marinade: mix the ginger in a shallow dish with the soy sauce, rice wine or sherry, sugar and five-spice powder. Add the monkfish and turn gently to coat. Cover and leave to marinate in the refrigerator for 1-2 hours, turning the fish occasionally.

When ready to cook, lift the pieces of fish out of the marinade with a slotted spoon and pat dry with kitchen paper. Reserve the marinade.

Lightly beat the egg whites in a shallow dish with the cornflour. Add the pieces of monkfish and turn gently to coat.

Pour the oil into the wok and heat over a moderate heat until hot but not smoking. shallow-fry the monkfish in batches in the hot oil, allowing 4-5 minutes for each batch or until the pieces of monkfish are golden on all sides. Lift the monkfish out with a slotted spoon, drain on kitchen paper and keep hot while shallow-frying the remainder.

Pour off all the oil from the wok, then wipe the wok clean with kitchen paper. Pour in the reserved marinade and the water and bring to the boil, stirring. Simmer for 1-2 minutes or until reduced slightly.

Arrange the fish on warmed individual plates and drizzle over the sauce. Serve at once, garnished with spring onion tassels, if you like.

Serves 3-4 as a main dish with accompaniments, or as part of an oriental meal

MUSSELS WITH CIDER

The wok makes an excellent pan for cooking mussels – its wide circumference lets you see at a glance when the shells are open. Dry cider makes a change from the white wine traditionally used for moules marinière, and it is less expensive. If you like, for a special occasion, you can stir a few spoonfuls of cream into the cider sauce before spooning over the mussels.

1 KG (2 LB) MUSSELS

300 ML (½ PINT) DRY CIDER

½ SMALL ONION, CHOPPED FINELY

1 CLOVE GARLIC, CHOPPED FINELY

1 BAY LEAF, TORN

1 TEASPOON RUBBED FRESH THYME OR ½ TEASPOON DRIED

25 G (1 OZ) BUTTER

PEPPER

CHOPPED PARSLEY TO GARNISH

CRUSTY FRENCH BREAD TO SERVE

Scrub the mussel shells under cold running water, scraping off the beards and barnacles with a small sharp knife. Put the mussels in a bowl of cold water and leave to soak for 20 minutes. Drain, then discard any mussels that are open or that do not close when tapped sharply against the work surface.

Pour the cider into the wok, add the onion, garlic, bay leaf, thyme, butter and pepper to taste and bring to the boil, stirring, until the butter has melted. Add the mussels, cover the wok and place over a high heat. Cook for 5 minutes or until the mussel shells open, shaking the wok frequently.

Divide the mussels equally between 4 warmed bowls, discarding any that are not open. Strain the cooking juices, spoon over the mussels and sprinkle with chopped parsley. Serve at once, with crusty French bread to mop up the juices.

Serves 4 as a starter

FISH BALLS WITH SWEET AND SOUR SAUCE

500 G (1 LB) WHITE FISH FILLETS, SKINNED AND
CHOPPED ROUGHLY

1 TABLESPOON FINELY CHOPPED FRESH CORIANDER

2 TEASPOONS SOY SAUCE

1 EGG WHITE

1 TABLESPOON CORNFLOUR

PEPPER

900 ML (1½ PINTS) FISH STOCK (SEE RIGHT)

2 TABLESPOONS SOY SAUCE

2 SPRING ONIONS, CHOPPED ROUGHLY

CHOPPED FRESH CORIANDER TO GARNISH

SAUCE:

2 TEASPOONS CORNFLOUR

2 TABLESPOONS WATER

2 TABLESPOONS SOY SAUCE

2 TABLESPOONS RICE WINE OR DRY SHERRY

1 TABLESPOON WINE VINEGAR (RED OR WHITE)

2 TEASPOONS TOMATO PURÉE

2 TEASPOONS SOFT BROWN SUGAR

Put the fish in a food processor, add the coriander, soy sauce, egg white, cornflour, and pepper to taste, then work until smooth and evenly mixed.

Turn the mixture into a bowl, then shape into about 36 small balls with hands dipped in cold water. Place the fish balls on a tray and chill in the refrigerator for about 30 minutes or until firm.

Meanwhile, prepare the sauce: mix the cornflour to a paste with the water, then stir in the remaining sauce ingredients. Set aside.

Pour the fish stock into the wok, add the soy sauce and spring onions and bring to the boil over a moderate heat. Lower the heat to a gentle simmer and drop in the fish balls. Poach for 6 minutes, then lift out with a slotted spoon and keep hot.

Pour off all but about 150 ml (¼ pint) stock from the wok. Stir the sauce to mix, then pour into the wok. Increase the heat to high and boil until thickened, stirring all the time. Return the fish balls to the wok and shake to coat in the sauce. Serve hot, sprinkled with chopped coriander.

Serves 4 as a main dish with accompaniments, or 6 as part of an oriental meal

FISH STOCK

UNLIKE MEAT AND CHICKEN STOCK, FISH STOCK IS QUICK TO PREPARE — AND WELL WORTH MAKING FOR THE EXTRA 'FISHY' FLAVOUR IT GIVES IN RECIPES WHERE FISH STOCK OR WATER IS CALLED FOR. DO NOT COOK IT FOR LONGER THAN THE TIME STATED OR IT WILL TASTE BITTER.

TO MAKE 900 ML (1½ PINTS) FISH STOCK, PUT 500 G (1 LB) WASHED FISH TRIMMINGS (HEADS, BONES AND SKIN, ETC) IN A LARGE SAUCEPAN WITH 900 ML (1½ PINTS) WATER, 2 TABLESPOONS EACH CHOPPED ONION AND CELERY, A HANDFUL OF PARSLEY STALKS, 2 BAY LEAVES, 1 TEASPOON PEPPERCORNS AND A SPLASH OR TWO OF DRY WHITE WINE IF YOU HAVE IT. BRING SLOWLY TO THE BOIL, THEN SKIM OFF ANY SCUM THAT RISES TO THE SURFACE WITH A SLOTTED SPOON. HALF COVER THE PAN WITH A LID AND SIMMER FOR 25 MINUTES, THEN STRAIN THE STOCK INTO A BOWL OR JUG. USE WITHIN 24 HOURS, KEEPING IT IN THE REFRIGERATOR IF NOT USING IMMEDIATELY, OR FREEZE FOR UP TO 3 MONTHS.

LEMON FRIED FISH WITH MUSHROOMS AND MANGETOUT

Monkfish has a wonderful flavour similar to lobster (it is often referred to as 'poor man's lobster') and its firm texture makes it ideal for stir-frying as it keeps its shape so well. In this recipe, button mushrooms and mangetout are used to help 'stretch' the monkfish and keep the cost down – although cheaper than lobster, monkfish is an expensive fish.

375 G (12 OZ) MONKFISH TAILS, SKINNED AND CUT INTO
BITE-SIZED PIECES

2 TABLESPOONS VEGETABLE OIL

2 TABLESPOONS SESAME OIL

250 G (8 OZ) BUTTON MUSHROOMS, SLICED

250 G (8 OZ) MANGETOUT, TOPS REMOVED

FLAT LEAF PARSLEY TO GARNISH

MARINADE:

2.5 CM (1 INCH) PIECE FRESH ROOT GINGER, PEELED AND
CHOPPED FINELY

1 CLOVE GARLIC, CRUSHED

3 TABLESPOONS SOY SAUCE

FINELY GRATED RIND AND JUICE OF 1 LARGE LEMON

½ TEASPOON FIVE-SPICE POWDER

First make the marinade: put the ginger and garlic in a shallow dish with the soy sauce, lemon rind and juice and five-spice powder. Add the monkfish and turn to coat. Cover and leave to marinate for about 30 minutes, turning the fish occasionally.

Heat the wok until hot. Add 1 tablespoon each of vegetable and sesame oil and heat over a moderate heat until hot. Add the mushrooms and mangetout and stir-fry for 3-4 minutes or until the juices run from the mushrooms. Tip the contents of the wok into a bowl and set aside.

Return the wok to the heat, add the remaining oils and heat until hot. With a slotted spoon, lift the monkfish out of the marinade and place in the wok. Stir-fry for 5 minutes, then return the mushrooms and mangetout to the wok with their juices and pour in the marinade. Increase the heat to high and toss until all the ingredients are combined and piping hot. Serve at once, garnished with sprigs of flat leaf parsley.

Serves 3-4 as a main dish with accompaniments, or as part of an oriental meal

FISH FILLETS IN SPICY TURMERIC AND COCONUT SAUCE

4 THICK HADDOCK FILLETS (TAKEN FROM THE CENTRE
OF THE FISH), SKINNED

JUICE OF 2 LIMES

2 TEASPOONS TURMERIC

1 SMALL ONION, CHOPPED ROUGHLY

1-2 CLOVES GARLIC, CHOPPED ROUGHLY

2 FRESH CHILLIES, SEEDED AND CHOPPED ROUGHLY

2 TEASPOONS GROUND CORIANDER

1 TEASPOON LAOS POWDER

ABOUT 300 ML (½ PINT) VEGETABLE OIL FOR
SHALLOW-FRYING

100 G (3½ OZ) CREAMED COCONUT, CHOPPED ROUGHLY

1 TEASPOON SOFT BROWN SUGAR

½ TEASPOON SALT

LIME WEDGES AND CHOPPED CHILLI TO GARNISH

Arrange the haddock fillets in a single layer in a shallow dish. Pour over the lime juice, then rub the turmeric into the flesh. Cover and leave to stand for about 20 minutes.

Meanwhile, in a food processor or mortar and pestle, work the onion, garlic and chillies to a paste with the coriander and laos powder, adding a little water if necessary. Set aside.

Heat the oil in the wok over a moderate heat until hot but not smoking. With a fish slice, lower 2 of the haddock fillets into the hot oil and shallow-fry for 5 minutes, taking care to keep them whole. Remove with the fish slice and drain on kitchen paper. Shallow-fry and drain the 2 remaining fillets in the same way.

Pour off all but 2 tablespoons oil from the wok. Add the spice paste and stir-fry over a gentle heat for 3-4 minutes. Add the chopped coconut, then pour in 300 ml (½ pint) boiling water and stir constantly until the coconut is dissolved. Add the sugar and salt and bring to the boil, stirring, then lower the heat and simmer until thickened, stirring frequently.

Return the haddock fillets to the wok and carefully spoon over the sauce, taking care to keep the pieces of fish whole. Heat through very gently, then transfer to warmed dinner plates with a fish slice. Spoon the coconut sauce over and around the fish and garnish with lime wedges and chopped chilli. Serve at once.

Serves 4 as a main dish, with accompaniments

QUICK-FRIED FISH IN YELLOW BEAN SAUCE

Yellow bean sauce is traditional with chicken in Chinese stir-fries, but it goes equally well with monkfish, as this recipe illustrates. The jars of yellow bean sauce sold in large supermarkets have an excellent flavour and are extremely useful for giving stir-fries an instant Chinese flavour, so it is well worth keeping a jar or two in the storecupboard.

500 G (1 LB) MONKFISH TAILS, SKINNED AND CUT INTO

CHUNKY PIECES

1 TABLESPOON VEGETABLE OIL

MARINADE:

4 TABLESPOONS FISH STOCK (SEE PAGE 29) OR

FISH STOCK MADE FROM A CUBE, OR WATER

3 TABLESPOONS SOY SAUCE

2 TABLESPOONS YELLOW BEAN SAUCE

1 TABLESPOON RICE WINE OR DRY SHERRY

1 TEASPOON CASTER SUGAR

First make the marinade: mix all the ingredients in a shallow dish, add the monkfish and turn gently to coat. Cover and leave to marinate in the refrigerator for 1-2 hours, turning the fish occasionally.

Heat the wok until hot. Add the oil and heat over a moderate heat until hot. Add the fish and its marinade, increase the heat to high and stir-fry for 4-5 minutes or until the fish is cooked. Serve at once.

Serves 3-4 as a main dish with accompaniments, or as part of an oriental meal

SEAFOOD STIR-FRY

White crab meat is excellent for Chinese stir-fries, but it is expensive. This recipe uses crab sticks, which are available from most large supermarkets and fishmongers and are much cheaper. They are a mixture of crab, white fish and flavourings and are perfect for stir-fries as they hold their shape well when cut into chunks and have a good strong crab flavour.

2 TABLESPOONS VEGETABLE OIL

1 MEDIUM GREEN PEPPER, CORED, SEEDED AND CUT INTO

LARGE DICE

2 CELERY STICKS, SLICED THINLY ON THE DIAGONAL

½ BUNCH SPRING ONIONS, SLICED THINLY ON THE DIAGONAL

12 CRAB STICKS, DEFROSTED AND DRIED THOROUGHLY, IF

FROZEN, CUT INTO LARGE CHUNKS

175 G (6 OZ) PEELED COOKED PRAWNS, DEFROSTED AND

DRIED THOROUGHLY, IF FROZEN

SAUCE:

2 TEASPOONS CORNFLOUR

4 TABLESPOONS WATER

2 TABLESPOONS SOY SAUCE

2 TABLESPOONS RICE WINE OR DRY SHERRY

1 TABLESPOON SOFT BROWN SUGAR

1 TABLESPOON TOMATO PURÉE

First prepare the sauce: mix the cornflour to a thin paste with the water, then stir in the remaining ingredients. Set aside.

Heat the wok until hot. Add the oil and heat over a moderate heat until hot. Add the green pepper and celery and stir-fry for 2-3 minutes or until just beginning to soften, taking care not to let them brown. Add the spring onions, crab and prawns, increase the heat to high and stir-fry for 2-3 minutes.

Stir the sauce to mix, pour into the wok and toss until all the ingredients are combined and piping hot.

Serves 2-3 as a main dish with accompaniments or as part of an oriental meal

STIR-FRIED PRAWNS WITH TOFU

Firm bean curd (tofu) can be bought in oriental stores. It is packed in brine, and is available loose by the piece or packed in plastic. Made from soya beans, it is high in protein yet low in fat. For a nutritious meal, serve this simple stir-fry over brown rice in Chinese bowls (see recipe for Nutty Brown Rice, right). If you are feeling extravagant, you could use raw 'tiger' prawn tails instead of the peeled cooked ones suggested here – simply increase the cooking time by a minute or two.

ABOUT 300 ML (½ PINT) VEGETABLE OIL FOR SHALLOW-FRYING

250 G (8 OZ) FIRM BEAN CURD (TOFU), DRAINED AND CUT INTO CUBES

250 G (8 OZ) PEELED COOKED PRAWNS, DEFROSTED AND DRIED THOROUGHLY, IF FROZEN

SAUCE:

2 TABLESPOONS SOY SAUCE

2 TABLESPOONS RICE WINE OR DRY SHERRY

1 TABLESPOON LEMON JUICE

1 TEASPOON CASTER SUGAR

2 TEASPOONS CORNFLOUR

100 ML (3½ FL OZ) FISH STOCK (SEE PAGE 29) OR FISH STOCK MADE FROM A CUBE

First prepare the sauce: put the soy sauce, rice wine or sherry and the lemon juice in a bowl or jug, add the sugar and cornflour and stir well to mix. Stir in the fish stock. Set aside.

Pour the oil into the wok and heat over a moderate heat until hot but not smoking. Add the bean curd and shallow-fry for 2-3 minutes or until golden on all sides, taking care not to let it break up. Lift out with a slotted spoon, drain and keep hot on kitchen paper.

Pour off all but about 1 tablespoon of the oil from the wok. Add the prawns, increase the heat to high and stir-fry for 1-2 minutes. Stir the sauce to mix, then pour into the wok. Bring to the boil, stirring, then add the bean curd and stir gently to mix with the prawns and coat in the sauce. Serve at once.

Serves 3-4 as a main dish, with rice as an accompaniment

NUTTY BROWN RICE

THIS MAKES A TASTY ACCOMPANIMENT TO SERVE WITH STIR-FRIES. IT COOKS BY ITSELF, LEAVING YOUR HANDS FREE FOR STIR-FRYING IN THE WOK.

HEAT 1 TABLESPOON OF VEGETABLE OIL AND A KNOB OF BUTTER IN A SAUCEPAN, ADD 1-2 TABLESPOONS OF FINELY CHOPPED ONION AND 2 CUPS OF BROWN RICE AND COOK OVER A MODERATE HEAT FOR 3-4 MINUTES OR UNTIL THE ONION SOFTENS AND THE RICE GLISTENS. POUR IN 5 CUPS OF HOT WATER (OR CHICKEN STOCK FOR EXTRA FLAVOUR) AND BRING TO THE BOIL. ADD SALT TO TASTE, STIR ONCE, THEN COVER AND SIMMER FOR 30-40 MINUTES OR UNTIL THE RICE IS TENDER AND ALL THE LIQUID IS ABSORBED (BROWN RICE WILL ALWAYS BE SLIGHTLY CHEWY). REMOVE FROM THE HEAT AND STIR IN 50 G (2 OZ) OF PINE NUTS OR CASHEWS, A KNOB OF BUTTER IF YOU LIKE, AND PLENTY OF FRESHLY GROUND BLACK PEPPER.

POULTRY

Lean, boneless chicken and turkey are two of the best meats for stir-frying. They cook in next to no time, are low in fat, and meltingly tender. Duck is a good choice for special occasions, with its rich 'gamey' flavour, but all three meats can be used interchangeably.

CHICKEN WITH CASHEWS

2 TABLESPOONS VEGETABLE OIL

4 SKINNED AND BONED CHICKEN BREASTS, EACH WEIGHING ABOUT 150 G (5 OZ), CUT INTO THIN STRIPS ACROSS THE GRAIN

1 BUNCH SPRING ONIONS, SLICED THINLY ON THE DIAGONAL

2 CLOVES GARLIC, CRUSHED

125 G (4 OZ) CASHEWS

PEPPER

BOILED OR STEAMED RICE TO SERVE

SAUCE:

2 TEASPOONS CORNFLOUR

6 TABLESPOONS COLD CHICKEN STOCK OR WATER

3 TABLESPOONS SOY SAUCE

2 TABLESPOONS RICE WINE OR DRY SHERRY

2 TEASPOONS DARK SOFT BROWN SUGAR

First prepare the sauce: mix the cornflour to a paste with 1 tablespoon of the stock or water, then stir in the remaining stock or water, the soy sauce, rice wine or sherry and sugar. Set aside.

Heat the wok until hot. Add the oil and heat over a moderate heat until hot. Add the chicken strips, increase the heat to high and stir-fry for 3-4 minutes or until lightly coloured on all sides, then add the spring onions and garlic. Stir-fry for a further minute.

Stir the sauce to mix, then pour into the wok. Bring to the boil, stirring constantly. Add the cashews and toss to combine with the chicken and spring onions. Add pepper to taste and serve at once with boiled or steamed rice.

Serves 3-4 as a main dish with accompaniments, or as part of an oriental meal

DUCK WITH SPICED ORANGE SAUCE

2 TABLESPOONS VEGETABLE OIL

4 DUCKLING BREAST FILLETS, EACH WEIGHING ABOUT 175 G (6 OZ), SKIN AND FAT REMOVED, CUT INTO THIN STRIPS ACROSS THE GRAIN

SEEDS OF 6 CARDAMOM PODS, CRUSHED

PEPPER

BOILED OR STEAMED RICE TO SERVE

ORANGE SEGMENTS TO GARNISH

SAUCE:

1 TABLESPOON CORNFLOUR

4 TABLESPOONS WATER

JUICE OF 1 LARGE ORANGE

1 TABLESPOON RICE WINE OR DRY SHERRY

1 TABLESPOON SOY SAUCE

1 TEASPOON DARK SOFT BROWN SUGAR

1 TEASPOON FIVE-SPICE POWDER

First prepare the sauce: mix the cornflour to a thin paste with the water, then stir in the orange juice, rice wine or sherry, soy sauce, sugar and five-spice powder. Set aside.

Heat the wok until hot. Add the oil and heat over a moderate heat until hot. Add the duck strips and crushed cardamom seeds, increase the heat to high and stir-fry for 3-4 minutes or until lightly coloured on all sides.

Stir the sauce to mix, then pour into the wok and bring to the boil, stirring. Stir-fry for a further 1-2 minutes or until the duck is tender and coated in the sauce. Add pepper to taste and serve at once with plain boiled or steamed rice, garnished with orange segments.

Serves 3-4 as a main dish with accompaniments, or as part of an oriental meal

DICED TURKEY WITH WALNUTS

This dish tastes so good no-one would guess it's low in calories and fat. If you happen to have ginger marmalade in the cupboard, you can use it instead of the orange marmalade and ground ginger suggested here.

JUICE OF **1** LARGE ORANGE

2 TABLESPOONS COARSE-CUT MARMALADE

2 TABLESPOONS SOY SAUCE

½ TEASPOON GROUND GINGER

2 TABLESPOONS WALNUT OIL

1 TABLESPOON VEGETABLE OIL

1 RED OR GREEN PEPPER, CORED, SEEDED AND DICED

50 G (**2** OZ) SHELLED WALNUTS

500 G (**1** LB) TURKEY BREAST FILLETS, DICED

PEPPER

ORANGE SLICES TO GARNISH

First mix the orange juice in a jug or bowl with the marmalade, soy sauce and ground ginger. Set aside.

Heat the wok until hot. Add the oils and heat over a moderate heat until hot. Add the diced pepper and the walnuts and stir-fry for 2-3 minutes. Remove the wok from the heat and transfer the pepper and walnuts to kitchen paper with a slotted spoon. Leave to drain.

Return the wok to the heat. Add the diced turkey, increase the heat to high and stir-fry for 3-4 minutes or until the turkey is lightly coloured on all sides. Add the orange mixture and stir well, adding a few tablespoons of water if there is not enough liquid.

Return the pepper and walnuts to the wok and toss for 30 seconds or until all the ingredients are combined and piping hot. Add pepper to taste and serve at once, garnished with orange slices.

Serves 3-4 as a main dish with accompaniments, or as part of an oriental meal

SPICED CHICKEN CURRY

Chicken thighs are available in packets in many large supermarkets. They are better for making curries than chicken breasts as their meat is more moist; they are also more economical. If you like a hot curry, leave some, or all, of the seeds in the chilli – the seeds are the hottest part.

1 CM (½ INCH) PIECE FRESH ROOT GINGER, PEELED AND CHOPPED ROUGHLY

1 CLOVE GARLIC, CHOPPED ROUGHLY

1 FRESH GREEN CHILLI, SEEDED AND CHOPPED ROUGHLY

2 TABLESPOONS VEGETABLE OIL

500 G (**1** LB) BONELESS CHICKEN THIGHS, SKINNED AND CUT INTO CHUNKS

1 TEASPOON TURMERIC

300 G (**10** OZ) RIPE TOMATOES, SKINNED AND CHOPPED ROUGHLY

50 G (**2** OZ) CREAMED COCONUT, GRATED

2 BAY LEAVES, TORN

2 CARDAMOM PODS, SPLIT

STRIP OF LEMON RIND

½ TEASPOON SALT

CHOPPED FRESH CORIANDER TO GARNISH

Pound the ginger, garlic and chilli in a mortar and pestle.

Heat the wok until hot. Add the oil and heat over a moderate heat until hot. Add the pounded mixture and stir-fry for 2-3 minutes, taking care not to let any of the ingredients brown. Add the chicken and turmeric, increase the heat to high and stir-fry for 3-4 minutes or until the chicken changes colour.

Add the tomatoes, grated creamed coconut, bay leaves, cardamom pods, lemon rind and salt and stir-fry until bubbling. Lower the heat to moderate and stir-fry for a further 10 minutes or until the chicken is tender and the sauce reduced. Remove and discard the bay leaves, cardamom pods and lemon rind. Serve at once, sprinkled with chopped coriander.

Serves 3-4 as a main dish, with accompaniments

INDONESIAN SATAY CHICKEN

Bottled chilli sauce is usually very hot and spicy, although strengths vary according to the brand. It is sold in supermarkets with oriental sections, as well as in oriental stores.

3 TABLESPOONS VEGETABLE OIL

1 SMALL ONION, CHOPPED FINELY

2.5 CM (1 INCH) PIECE FRESH ROOT GINGER, PEELED AND CHOPPED FINELY

1 CLOVE GARLIC, CRUSHED

500 G (1 LB) BONELESS CHICKEN THIGHS, SKINNED AND CUT INTO BITE-SIZED PIECES

1 TEASPOON CHILLI POWDER, OR TO TASTE

2 TABLESPOONS CRUNCHY PEANUT BUTTER

2 TABLESPOONS CHILLI SAUCE

100 G (3½ OZ) CREAMED COCONUT, CHOPPED ROUGHLY

300 ML (½ PINT) HOT WATER

1 TEASPOON DARK SOFT BROWN SUGAR

¼ TEASPOON SALT

Heat the wok until hot. Add the oil and heat over a moderate heat until hot. Add the onion, ginger and garlic and stir-fry for 2-3 minutes or until softened, taking care not to let the ingredients brown.

Add the chicken pieces, increase the heat to high and stir-fry for 3-4 minutes or until lightly coloured on all sides. Sprinkle in the chilli powder, add the peanut butter and chilli sauce and stir to mix.

Add the creamed coconut a few pieces at a time and stir-fry until melted. Gradually add the hot water and bring to the boil, stirring all the time. Add the sugar and salt, then continue stir-frying for about 5 minutes or until the sauce is thickened. Serve hot.

Serves 3-4 as a main dish with accompaniments, or as part of an oriental meal

CHAIRMAN MAO'S CHICKEN

Chairman Mao was very fond of hot and spicy food. This recipe uses fresh chillies and chilli sauce, and so is named after him. For a really hot flavour, include some, or all, of the seeds from the chillies.

2 EGG WHITES

2 TABLESPOONS CORNFLOUR

4 SKINNED AND BONED CHICKEN BREASTS, EACH WEIGHING ABOUT 150 G (5 OZ), CUT INTO THIN STRIPS ACROSS THE GRAIN

ABOUT 600 ML (1 PINT) VEGETABLE OIL FOR DEEP-FRYING

250 G (8 OZ) CARROTS, CUT INTO JULIENNE STRIPS

3 CELERY STICKS, SLICED THINLY ON THE DIAGONAL

3 SPRING ONIONS, SLICED THINLY ON THE DIAGONAL

2.5 CM (1 INCH) PIECE FRESH ROOT GINGER, PEELED AND CUT INTO JULIENNE STRIPS

2 CLOVES GARLIC, CHOPPED FINELY

2 FRESH CHILLIES, SEEDED AND CHOPPED FINELY

150 ML (¼ PINT) CHICKEN STOCK OR WATER

2 TABLESPOONS CHILLI SAUCE

1 TABLESPOON RICE WINE OR DRY SHERRY

1 TEASPOON SOFT BROWN SUGAR

¼ TEASPOON SALT

Lightly beat the egg whites in a shallow dish with the cornflour. Add the chicken and turn to coat. Set aside.

Pour the oil for deep-frying into the wok and heat to 180°C-190°C, 350°F-375°F, or until a cube of bread browns in 30 seconds. One at a time, lift the chicken strips out of the egg mixture with a fork and drop into the hot oil. Deep-fry in batches for 3-4 minutes or until golden and tender. Lift out with a slotted spoon and drain on kitchen paper while deep-frying the remainder.

Pour off all but 2 tablespoons oil from the wok. Add all the vegetables, the ginger, garlic and chillies and stir-fry over a moderate heat for 2-3 minutes, then add the chicken stock or water, the chilli sauce, rice wine or sherry, sugar and salt. Stir for a further 2 minutes, or until the carrots are just tender.

Return the chicken to the wok and stir for 1-2 minutes or until all the ingredients are well combined and piping hot. Serve at once.

Serves 3-4 as a main dish with accompaniments, or as part of an oriental meal

PLUM DUCK

2 TABLESPOONS VEGETABLE OIL

4 DUCKLING BREAST FILLETS, EACH WEIGHING ABOUT

175 G (6 OZ), SKIN AND FAT REMOVED, CUT INTO THIN

STRIPS ACROSS THE GRAIN

250 G (8 OZ) RED PLUMS, STONED AND SLICED THINLY

FINELY GRATED RIND AND JUICE OF 1 LARGE ORANGE

2 TABLESPOONS PORT

2 TABLESPOONS RED WINE VINEGAR

2 TEASPOONS SOFT BROWN SUGAR

¼ TEASPOON GROUND CINNAMON

SALT AND PEPPER

THYME SPRIGS TO GARNISH

Heat the wok until hot. Add the oil and heat over a moderate heat until hot. Add the duck strips, increase the heat to high and stir-fry for 3-4 minutes or until lightly coloured on all sides. Remove the wok from the heat and transfer the duck to a plate with a slotted spoon. Set aside.

Return the wok to a moderate heat. Add the plums, orange rind and juice, port, wine vinegar, sugar, cinnamon and salt and pepper to taste. Stir-fry for 5 minutes, then return the duck and its juices to the wok and increase the heat to high. Toss for 1-2 minutes or until all the ingredients are combined and piping hot. Taste for seasoning and serve at once, garnished with sprigs of thyme.

Serves 3-4 as a main dish with accompaniments, or as part of an oriental meal

RIBBONS OF DUCK WITH CHERRIES

Cherries and duck are a natural combination – the sweetness of the fruit is the perfect complement to the richness of the meat. The acidity of the lemon juice adds bite to the sauce.

1 TABLESPOON ARROWROOT

4 TABLESPOONS WATER

2 TABLESPOONS VEGETABLE OIL

4 DUCKLING BREAST FILLETS, EACH WEIGHING ABOUT

175 G (6 OZ), SKIN AND FAT REMOVED, CUT INTO THIN

STRIPS ACROSS THE GRAIN

1 MEDIUM RED-SKINNED ONION, SLICED THINLY

2.5 CM (1 INCH) PIECE FRESH ROOT GINGER, PEELED AND

CUT INTO JULIENNE STRIPS

1 X 450 G (1 LB) CAN PITTED DARK SWEET CHERRIES,

DRAINED WITH 4 TABLESPOONS JUICE RESERVED

FINELY GRATED RIND AND JUICE OF ½ LEMON

SALT AND PEPPER

FLAT LEAF PARSLEY SPRIGS TO GARNISH

First mix the arrowroot to a thin paste with the water in a jug or bowl. Set aside.

Heat the wok until hot. Add the oil and heat over a moderate heat until hot. Add the duck strips, increase the heat to high and stir-fry for 3-4 minutes or until lightly coloured on all sides. Remove the wok from the heat and transfer the duck to a plate with a slotted spoon. Set aside.

Return the wok to a moderate heat. Add the onion and ginger and stir-fry for 2-3 minutes or until softened, taking care not to let them brown. Add the reserved cherry juice, the lemon rind and juice and salt and pepper to taste. Bring to the boil, stirring, then add the arrowroot paste and stir until the sauce thickens.

Return the duck and its juices to the wok, add the cherries and increase the heat to high. Toss for 1-2 minutes or until all the ingredients are combined and piping hot. Taste for seasoning and serve at once, garnished with flat leaf parsley.

Serves 3-4 as a main dish with accompaniments, or as part of an oriental meal

CHICKEN CHOP SUEY

*The name chop suey comes from the Chinese word 'zasui'
meaning 'mixed bits'. The choice of meat and vegetables for
a chop suey can vary according to what is available, making
it the ideal dish for using up leftovers and vegetables from the
freezer. Try to use at least one seasonal vegetable, however,
to give the chop suey a fresh flavour.*

3 TABLESPOONS VEGETABLE OIL

1 SMALL ONION, CHOPPED FINELY

3 MEDIUM CARROTS, CUT INTO JULIENNE STRIPS

1 GREEN PEPPER, CORED, SEEDED AND CUT INTO
JULIENNE STRIPS

125 G (4 OZ) FROZEN PEAS

75 G (3 OZ) FROZEN SWEETCORN KERNELS

150 ML (¼ PINT) CHICKEN STOCK

250-375 G (8-12 OZ) COOKED CHICKEN MEAT, SKINNED AND
CUT INTO STRIPS

75 G (3 OZ) BEAN SPROUTS

PEPPER

SAUCE:

2 TEASPOONS CORNFLOUR

4 TABLESPOONS WATER

3 TABLESPOONS SOY SAUCE

2 TABLESPOONS RICE WINE OR DRY SHERRY

1 TABLESPOON WINE VINEGAR (RED OR WHITE)

2 TEASPOONS SOFT BROWN SUGAR

First prepare the sauce: mix the cornflour to a thin paste with
the water, then stir in the soy sauce, rice wine or sherry, wine
vinegar and sugar. Set aside.

Heat the wok until hot. Add the oil and heat over a
moderate heat until hot. Add the onion and carrots and stir-
fry for 2 minutes, then add the green pepper and stir-fry for a
further 2 minutes. Add the peas and sweetcorn, toss well to
mix, then pour in the chicken stock and bring to the boil,
stirring. Simmer for 3-4 minutes, stirring frequently.

Stir the sauce to mix, pour into the wok and increase the
heat to high. Stir constantly until thickened.

Add the chicken and bean sprouts and toss for about
2 minutes or until evenly combined and piping hot. Add
pepper to taste and serve at once.

Serves 3-4 as a main dish

DEVILLED CHICKEN LIVERS WITH GINGER

2 TABLESPOONS VEGETABLE OIL

5 CM (2 INCH) PIECE FRESH ROOT GINGER, PEELED AND CUT
INTO JULIENNE STRIPS

½ BUNCH SPRING ONIONS, SLICED THINLY ON THE DIAGONAL

250 G (8 OZ) CHICKEN LIVERS, SLICED

SALT AND PEPPER

SAUCE:

1 TABLESPOON CORNFLOUR

6 TABLESPOONS WATER

1 TABLESPOON TOMATO PURÉE

2 TEASPOONS WORCESTERSHIRE SAUCE

2 TEASPOONS LEMON JUICE

1 TEASPOON PREPARED MUSTARD

First prepare the sauce: mix the cornflour to a thin paste with
the water, then stir in the remaining ingredients. Set aside.

Heat the wok until hot. Add the oil and heat over a
moderate heat until hot. Add the ginger and spring onions
and stir-fry for 2-3 minutes or until softened, taking care not
to let them brown. Add the chicken livers and stir-fry for a
further 2 minutes or until they lose their pink colour.

Stir the sauce to mix, then pour into the wok. Stir-fry for a
further 5 minutes or until the livers are cooked but still pink
in the centre. Add salt and pepper to taste and serve at once.

Serves 3-4 as a main dish with accompaniments, or as part of
an oriental meal

DICED CHICKEN IN BLACK BEAN SAUCE

Try to make the diced chicken, peppers and celery the same size so the finished dish will look attractive. Black bean sauce, made from salted black beans, is available in jars from the oriental sections of large supermarkets.

4 TABLESPOONS VEGETABLE OIL

2.5 CM (1 INCH) PIECE FRESH ROOT GINGER, PEELED AND CHOPPED VERY FINELY

1 CLOVE GARLIC, CRUSHED

3 CELERY STICKS, DICED

1 SMALL GREEN PEPPER, CORED, SEEDED AND DICED

1 SMALL RED PEPPER, CORED, SEEDED AND DICED

4 SKINNED AND BONED CHICKEN BREASTS, EACH WEIGHING ABOUT 150 G (5 OZ), DICED

4 TABLESPOONS BLACK BEAN SAUCE

4 TABLESPOONS CHICKEN STOCK OR WATER

SALT AND PEPPER

Heat the wok until hot. Add 2 tablespoons of the oil and heat over a moderate heat until hot. Add the ginger and garlic and stir-fry for 2-3 minutes, taking care not to let them brown. Add the celery and green and red peppers and stir-fry for a further 2-3 minutes or until the peppers are just beginning to soften. Remove the wok from the heat and tip the vegetables into a bowl. Set aside.

Return the wok to the heat, add the remaining oil and heat until hot. Add the diced chicken, increase the heat to high and stir-fry for 3-4 minutes or until lightly coloured on all sides. Add the black bean sauce and the chicken stock or water and stir to mix.

Return the vegetables to the wok and toss for 1-2 minutes or until all the ingredients are combined and piping hot. Add salt and pepper to taste and serve at once.

Serves 3-4 as a main dish with accompaniments, or as part of an oriental meal

TURKEY WITH PIQUANT PEPPER SAUCE

This sauce, with its chillies, Szechuan peppercorns and garlic, is not for the faint-hearted! Szechuan peppercorns are available from the spice racks of large supermarkets. It gives a tangy, almost citrus, flavour to Chinese food.

1 TABLESPOON SZECHUAN PEPPERCORNS

3 TABLESPOONS VEGETABLE OIL

500 G (1 LB) TURKEY BREAST FILLETS, CUT INTO THIN STRIPS ACROSS THE GRAIN

3 DRIED RED CHILLIES, CHOPPED FINELY

3 CLOVES GARLIC, CRUSHED

5 CM (2 INCH) PIECE FRESH ROOT GINGER, PEELED AND CHOPPED VERY FINELY

SAUCE:

4 TEASPOONS CORNFLOUR

8 TABLESPOONS COLD CHICKEN STOCK OR WATER

2 TABLESPOONS WHITE WINE VINEGAR

2 TABLESPOONS SOY SAUCE

1 TABLESPOON CHILLI SAUCE

2 TEASPOONS SOFT BROWN SUGAR

2 TEASPOONS TOMATO PURÉE

First prepare the sauce: mix the cornflour to a paste with 2 tablespoons of the stock or water, then stir in the remaining stock or water and the remaining ingredients. Set aside.

Heat the wok until hot. Add the Szechuan pepper and dry-fry over a gentle heat for 1-2 minutes. Remove from the wok and crush in a mortar and pestle.

Heat 2 tablespoons of the oil in the wok over a moderate heat until hot. Add the turkey and Szechuan pepper, increase the heat to high and stir-fry for 3-4 minutes or until lightly coloured on all sides. Remove the wok from the heat and transfer the turkey to a plate with a slotted spoon. Set aside.

Return the wok to a moderate heat, add the remaining oil and heat until hot. Add the chillies, garlic and ginger and stir-fry for 2-3 minutes or until softened, taking care not to let the ingredients brown.

Stir the sauce to mix, pour into the wok and increase the heat to high. Stir-fry for a few minutes until the sauce is thickened, then return the turkey and its juices to the wok and toss for 1-2 minutes or until all the ingredients are combined and piping hot. Serve at once.

Serves 3-4 as a main dish with accompaniments, or as part of an oriental meal

LEMON CHICKEN

*This classic dish, which originated in Hong Kong, is
simplicity itself to make. Spring onions are included to add
crunch to the dish, but they are not essential. If you prefer,
you can use green pepper instead, or leave out the
vegetables altogether.*

1 EGG WHITE

2 TEASPOONS CORNFLOUR

PINCH OF SALT

2 SKINNED AND BONED CHICKEN BREASTS, EACH WEIGHING
ABOUT 150 G (5 OZ), CUT INTO THIN STRIPS ACROSS
THE GRAIN

300 ML (½ PINT) VEGETABLE OIL FOR SHALLOW-FRYING

½ BUNCH SPRING ONIONS, SHREDDED

1 CLOVE GARLIC, CRUSHED

LEMON SLICES TO GARNISH

SAUCE:

2 TEASPOONS CORNFLOUR

4 TABLESPOONS COLD CHICKEN STOCK OR WATER

FINELY GRATED RIND OF ½ LEMON

2 TABLESPOONS LEMON JUICE

1 TABLESPOON SOY SAUCE

2 TEASPOONS RICE WINE OR DRY SHERRY

2 TEASPOONS CASTER SUGAR

First prepare the sauce: mix the cornflour to a thin paste with
the stock or water, then stir in the remaining sauce
ingredients. Set aside.

Lightly beat the egg white in a shallow dish with the
cornflour and salt. Add the strips of chicken and turn to coat.
Set aside.

Heat the oil in the wok until hot but not smoking. One at a
time, lift the strips of chicken out of the egg white mixture
with a fork and drop into the hot oil. Shallow-fry in batches
for about 3-4 minutes at a time or until golden. Lift out with a
slotted spoon and drain on kitchen paper. Keep hot.

Pour off all but 1 tablespoon oil from the wok. Add the
spring onions and garlic and stir-fry over a moderate heat for
30 seconds. Stir the sauce to mix, pour into the wok, increase
the heat to high and bring to the boil, stirring constantly.

Return the chicken to the wok and stir-fry for 1-2 minutes
or until evenly coated in the sauce. Serve at once, garnished
with lemon slices.

Serves 2 as a main dish with accompaniments, or as part of an
oriental meal

MALAYSIAN ORANGE CHICKEN

2 EGG WHITES

2 TABLESPOONS CORNFLOUR

4 SKINNED AND BONED CHICKEN BREASTS, EACH WEIGHING
ABOUT 150 G (5 OZ), CUT INTO THIN STRIPS ACROSS
THE GRAIN

ABOUT 300 ML (½ PINT) VEGETABLE OIL FOR
SHALLOW-FRYING

1 BUNCH SPRING ONIONS, SLICED THINLY ON THE DIAGONAL

125 G (4 OZ) FROZEN PEAS

SALT AND PEPPER

SAUCE:

175 ML (6 FL OZ) FRESH ORANGE JUICE

4 TABLESPOONS CONCENTRATED ORANGE SQUASH

2 TABLESPOONS SOY SAUCE

1 TABLESPOON CIDER VINEGAR

1 TEASPOON SOFT BROWN SUGAR

TO GARNISH:

ORANGE SLICES

FLAT LEAF PARSLEY

Lightly beat the egg whites with the cornflour and a pinch of
salt in a shallow dish. Add the strips of chicken and turn to
coat. Set the dish aside.

Mix all the sauce ingredients together in a jug or bowl and
then set aside.

Heat the oil in the wok until hot but not smoking. One at a
time, lift the strips of chicken out of the egg white mixture
with a fork and drop into the hot oil. Shallow-fry in batches
for about 3-4 minutes at a time or until golden. Lift out with a
slotted spoon and drain on kitchen paper. Keep hot.

Pour off all but about 2 tablespoons oil from the wok. Add
the spring onions and stir-fry over a moderate heat for
30 seconds. Pour in the sauce and bring to the boil, stirring,
then add the peas and salt and pepper to taste and simmer,
stirring frequently, for about 5 minutes or until cooked.

Return the chicken to the wok and toss for 1-2 minutes or
until all the ingredients are evenly combined and piping hot.
Serve at once, garnished with orange slices and flat
leaf parsley.

Serves 3-4 as a main dish with accompaniments, or as part of
an oriental meal

DEEP-FRIED CHINESE CHICKEN

Enclosed in a crisp and crunchy batter, these tender cubes of marinated chicken have a fragrant flavour when bitten into. Serve them as a starter, with bowls of soy sauce for dipping or, if you like, you can spear each cube with a cocktail stick and serve them with pre-dinner drinks.

500 G (1 LB) SKINNED AND BONED CHICKEN BREASTS, CUT
INTO 2.5 CM (1 INCH) CHUNKS

125 G (4 OZ) PLAIN FLOUR

PINCH OF SALT

2 EGGS

100 ML (3½ FL OZ) WATER

ABOUT 600 ML (1 PINT) VEGETABLE OIL FOR DEEP-FRYING

SOY SAUCE FOR DIPPING

MARINADE:

2 TABLESPOONS SOY SAUCE

2 TABLESPOONS RICE WINE OR DRY SHERRY

2.5 CM (1 INCH) PIECE FRESH ROOT GINGER, PEELED
AND CRUSHED

2 SPRING ONIONS, CHOPPED VERY FINELY

1 CLOVE GARLIC, CRUSHED

2 TEASPOONS CASTER SUGAR

First make the marinade: mix all the ingredients together in a shallow dish, add the chunks of chicken and turn to coat. Cover the dish and leave to marinate in the refrigerator for at least 4 hours, preferably overnight, turning the chunks of chicken occasionally.

When ready to cook, make the batter: sift the flour and salt into a bowl, make a well in the centre and add the eggs. Beat well to mix, adding the water a little at a time until a smooth, coating batter is formed.

Drain the chicken in a sieve, discarding the marinade.

Pour the oil into the wok and heat to 190°C, 375°F, or until a cube of bread browns in 20-30 seconds. Drop about one-quarter of the marinated chicken into the batter and mix to coat. With a fork, lift the chunks of chicken out of the batter one at a time and immediately drop into the hot oil. Deep-fry for 5-6 minutes or until crisp and light golden, then lift out with a slotted spoon and place on kitchen paper to drain. Keep hot in the oven while deep-frying the remaining batches of chicken, one-quarter at a time. Serve at once, with soy sauce handed separately for dipping.

Serves 6 as a starter

SOY CHICKEN

This recipe is unbelievably simple. Provided you have time to let the chicken marinate for at least 4 hours before cooking, there is very little else to do in the way of preparation.

500 G (1 LB) BONELESS CHICKEN THIGHS, SKINNED AND CUT
INTO 2.5 CM (1 INCH) CHUNKS

MARINADE AND SAUCE:

3 TABLESPOONS LIGHT SOY SAUCE

3 TABLESPOONS DARK SOY SAUCE

2 TABLESPOONS RED WINE VINEGAR

2 TABLESPOONS DARK SOFT BROWN SUGAR

2 TEASPOONS TOMATO PURÉE

1 CLOVE GARLIC, CRUSHED

1-2 TEASPOONS CHILLI POWDER, ACCORDING TO TASTE

First make the marinade: put all the ingredients in a shallow dish, add the chicken and turn to coat. Cover and leave to marinate in the refrigerator for 4 hours or overnight, turning the chicken occasionally.

When ready to cook, drain the chicken, pouring the marinade into the wok. Place the wok over a moderate heat and stir the marinade until bubbling. Add the chicken pieces, stir to mix with the marinade, then simmer, stirring frequently, for about 10 minutes or until the chicken is tender and the sauce reduced. Serve hot.

Serves 3-4 as a main dish with accompaniments, or as part of an oriental meal

TURKEY WITH COCONUT, GINGER AND LIME

500 G (1 LB) TURKEY BREAST FILLETS, CUT INTO THIN STRIPS
ACROSS THE GRAIN

100 G (3½ OZ) CREAMED COCONUT, CHOPPED ROUGHLY

2 TABLESPOONS VEGETABLE OIL

JUICE OF **½** LIME

PEPPER

MARINADE:

2.5 CM (1 INCH) PIECE FRESH ROOT GINGER, PEELED
AND CRUSHED

1 CLOVE GARLIC, CRUSHED

FINELY GRATED RIND AND JUICE OF **½** LIME

2 TABLESPOONS SOY SAUCE

2 TEASPOONS LIGHT SOFT BROWN SUGAR

TO GARNISH:

LIME SLICES

CHOPPED FRESH CORIANDER LEAVES

First make the marinade: mix all the marinade ingredients together in a shallow dish, add the turkey strips and turn to coat. Cover and set aside for at least 20 minutes.

Meanwhile, make the coconut milk: put the chopped coconut in a measuring jug, pour in boiling water up to the 300 ml (½ pint) mark and stir until the coconut is dissolved. Set aside.

Heat the wok until hot. Add the oil and heat over a moderate heat until hot. Add the turkey and its marinade and stir-fry for 3-4 minutes or until lightly coloured on all sides.

Add half of the coconut milk and bring to the boil, stirring, then stir-fry for a few minutes.

Lift the turkey out of the sauce with a slotted spoon, arrange on a warmed serving platter, cover and keep hot.

Pour the remaining coconut milk into the wok, then add the lime juice. Increase the heat to high and bring to the boil. Stir for a few minutes longer or until the sauce is thickened. Add pepper to taste, then pour over the turkey. Garnish with lime slices and coriander leaves and serve at once.

Serves 3-4 as a main dish, with accompaniments

COCONUT MILK

COCONUT MILK IS NOT THE LIQUID IN THE CENTRE OF A COCONUT, BUT THE TERM USED TO DESCRIBE THE MILKY LIQUID OBTAINED BY STEEPING COCONUT IN WATER. IT IS USED FREQUENTLY IN SOUTH-EAST ASIAN COOKING TO ADD RICHNESS AND FLAVOUR TO SAVOURY DISHES.

BLOCKS OF SOLID CREAMED COCONUT SOLD IN SUPERMARKETS ARE CONVENIENT FOR MAKING 'INSTANT' COCONUT MILK, BUT HERE IS A METHOD FOR MAKING COCONUT MILK YOURSELF AT HOME.

GRATE THE FLESH FROM HALF A FRESH COCONUT OR USE 175 G (6 OZ) DESICCATED COCONUT AND PLACE IN A HEATPROOF BOWL. POUR OVER 450 ML (¾ PINT) BOILING WATER, STIR, THEN LEAVE TO SOAK FOR 30 MINUTES. STRAIN THE LIQUID THROUGH A FINE SIEVE, PRESSING THE COCONUT HARD WITH THE BACK OF A METAL SPOON TO EXTRACT AS MUCH OF THE LIQUID AS POSSIBLE.

CHICKEN WITH MANGETOUT

5-15 G (¼-½ OZ) DRIED SHIITAKE MUSHROOMS, SOAKED IN

WARM WATER FOR 20 MINUTES

2 TEASPOONS CORNFLOUR

150 ML (¼ PINT) COLD CHICKEN STOCK

5 TABLESPOONS OLIVE OIL

4 SKINNED AND BONED CHICKEN BREASTS, EACH WEIGHING

ABOUT 150 G (5 OZ), CUT INTO STRIPS

ACROSS THE GRAIN

150 G (5 OZ) MANGETOUT, TOPS REMOVED

1 MEDIUM ONION, CHOPPED FINELY

2 CLOVES GARLIC, CRUSHED

125 G (4 OZ) BROWN CAP MUSHROOMS, SLICED THINLY

4 TABLESPOONS DRY SHERRY

FINELY GRATED RIND AND JUICE OF ½ LEMON

3 TABLESPOONS FINELY CHOPPED PARSLEY

SALT AND PEPPER

Drain the dried mushrooms and reserve the soaking liquid. Slice the mushrooms thinly. Mix the cornflour to a paste with 1-2 tablespoons of the stock, then stir in the rest. Set aside.

Heat the wok until hot. Add half the olive oil and heat over a moderate heat until hot. Add the chicken strips, increase the heat to high and stir-fry for 3-4 minutes or until lightly coloured on all sides. Remove the wok from the heat and transfer the chicken to a bowl with a slotted spoon. Set aside.

Return the wok to a moderate heat, add 1 tablespoon of the remaining oil and heat until hot. Add the mangetout and stir-fry for 2-3 minutes. Remove the wok from the heat and transfer the mangetout to the bowl with the chicken.

Return the wok to the heat, add the remaining oil and heat until hot. Add the onion and stir-fry for 2-3 minutes until softened, taking care not to let it brown. Add the dried mushrooms, garlic and fresh mushrooms, increase the heat to high and stir-fry for 5 minutes, tossing the ingredients in the wok until the juices run from the mushrooms.

Stir the cornflour mixture, then pour into the wok and bring to the boil, stirring all the time. Add the reserved soaking liquid from the dried mushrooms, the sherry, lemon rind and juice, and salt and pepper to taste. Simmer for 2-3 minutes or until thickened and slightly reduced, stirring frequently.

Return the chicken and mangetout to the wok and toss 1-2 minutes or until all the ingredients are combined and piping hot. Add the parsley, taste for seasoning and serve.

Serves 3-4 as a main dish with accompaniments, or as part of an oriental meal

ORIENTAL CHICKEN WITH TURMERIC

Macadamia nuts are noted for their rich flavour and waxy texture. Be sure to buy the unsalted ones for this recipe. Serai or sereh powder is dried lemon grass, a convenient way of adding this lovely citrus flavour to oriental curries and stir-fries. Like other dried herbs it should be stored in its jar in a cool, dark place. If you are lucky enough to be able to get fresh lemon grass, however, you can use it instead of the serai powder and lemon rind in this dish. You will need 1 stem lemon grass, bruised.

100 G (3½ OZ) CREAMED COCONUT, CHOPPED ROUGHLY

50 G (2 OZ) MACADAMIA NUTS, CHOPPED ROUGHLY

1 CLOVE GARLIC, CHOPPED ROUGHLY

3 TABLESPOONS VEGETABLE OIL

1 MEDIUM ONION, CHOPPED FINELY

8 BONELESS CHICKEN THIGHS, SKINNED AND CUT INTO

LARGE CHUNKS

1 TABLESPOON TURMERIC

1 TEASPOON SERAI POWDER

THINLY PARED RIND AND JUICE OF 1 LEMON

SALT AND PEPPER

FLAT LEAF PARSLEY TO GARNISH

First make the coconut milk: put the chopped coconut in a measuring jug, pour in boiling water up to the 300 ml (½ pint) mark and stir until the coconut is dissolved. Set aside.

Pound half of the macadamia nuts to a paste with the garlic in a mortar and pestle. Heat the wok until hot. Add the oil and heat over a moderate heat until hot. Add the onion together with the nut and garlic paste and stir-fry for 2-3 minutes or until the onion is softened, taking care not to let the ingredients brown.

Add the chicken pieces, increase the heat to high and stir-fry for 1-2 minutes or until the chicken is lightly coloured on all sides. Stir in the turmeric and serai powder and salt and pepper to taste. Add the coconut milk and bring to the boil, stirring constantly.

Lower the heat, add the lemon rind and juice and simmer for about 10 minutes or until the chicken is tender and the sauce thickened, stirring frequently to prevent sticking. Remove and discard the lemon rind. Taste for seasoning and serve hot, sprinkled with the remaining chopped macadamia nuts, and flat leaf parsley sprigs.

Serves 3-4 as a main dish with accompaniments, or as part of an oriental meal

STIR-FRIED CHICKEN WITH CRUNCHY VEGETABLES

3 TABLESPOONS VEGETABLE OIL

500 G (1 LB) SKINNED AND BONED CHICKEN BREASTS, CUT INTO THIN STRIPS ACROSS THE GRAIN

125 G (4 OZ) WHITE CABBAGE, SHREDDED FINELY

125 G (4 OZ) BEAN SPROUTS

1 LARGE GREEN PEPPER, CORED, SEEDED AND CUT LENGTHWAYS INTO THIN STRIPS

2 MEDIUM CARROTS, CUT INTO JULIENNE STRIPS

2 CLOVES GARLIC, CRUSHED

PEPPER

SAUCE:

2 TEASPOONS CORNFLOUR

4 TABLESPOONS WATER

3 TABLESPOONS SOY SAUCE

First prepare the sauce: mix the cornflour to a thin paste with the water, then stir in the soy sauce. Set aside.

Heat the wok until hot. Add 2 tablespoons of the oil and heat over a moderate heat until hot. Add the chicken strips, increase the heat to high and stir-fry for 3-4 minutes or until lightly coloured on all sides.

Remove the wok from the heat and transfer the chicken to a plate with a slotted spoon. Set aside.

Return the wok to a moderate heat, add the remaining oil and heat until hot. Add all the vegetables and the garlic and stir-fry for 2-3 minutes or until the green pepper is just beginning to soften.

Stir the sauce to mix, then pour into the wok. Increase the heat to high and toss the ingredients until the sauce thickens and coats the vegetables. Add the chicken with its juices and toss for 1-2 minutes or until all the ingredients are combined and piping hot. Add pepper to taste and serve at once.

Serves 3-4 as a main dish with accompaniments, or as part of an oriental meal

TURKEY WITH THREE PEPPERS

Peppers are often sold in packs of three in supermarkets. The combination of green, red and yellow is appealing, although orange and purple peppers could also be used as these are becoming more widely available.

3 TABLESPOONS VEGETABLE OIL

500 G (1 LB) TURKEY BREAST FILLETS, CUT INTO THIN STRIPS ACROSS THE GRAIN

3 LARGE PEPPERS (1 GREEN, 1 RED, 1 YELLOW), CORED, SEEDED AND CUT LENGTHWAYS INTO THIN STRIPS

4 SPRING ONIONS, SLICED THINLY ON THE DIAGONAL

1 CLOVE GARLIC, CRUSHED

PEPPER

SAUCE:

1 TABLESPOON CORNFLOUR

6 TABLESPOONS COLD CHICKEN STOCK OR WATER

2 TABLESPOONS RICE WINE OR DRY SHERRY

2 TABLESPOONS SOY SAUCE

1 TABLESPOON LEMON JUICE

½ TEASPOON GROUND GINGER

First prepare the sauce: mix the cornflour to a paste with 2 tablespoons of the stock or water, then stir in the remaining stock or water, the rice wine or sherry, soy sauce, lemon juice and ginger Set aside.

Heat the wok until hot. Add 2 tablespoons of the oil and heat over a moderate heat until hot. Add the turkey strips, increase the heat to high and stir-fry for 3-4 minutes or until lightly coloured on all sides. Remove the wok from the heat and transfer the turkey strips to a plate with a slotted spoon. Set aside.

Return the wok to a moderate heat, add the remaining oil and heat until hot. Add the peppers, spring onions and garlic and stir-fry for 2-3 minutes or until the peppers are just beginning to soften, tossing them well to combine.

Stir the sauce to mix, then pour into the wok. Increase the heat to high and stir vigorously for 1-2 minutes. Return the turkey strips and its juices to the wok and toss until evenly combined and piping hot. Add the pepper to taste and serve at once.

Serves 4 as a main dish with accompaniments, or as part of an oriental meal

CHICKEN WITH GREEN BEANS AND PINE KERNELS

250 G (8 OZ) GREEN BEANS, TOPPED AND TAILED AND CUT

IN HALF

4 TABLESPOONS VEGETABLE OIL

50-75 G (2-3 OZ) PINE KERNELS

4 SKINNED AND BONED CHICKEN BREASTS, EACH WEIGHING

ABOUT 150 G (5 OZ), CUT INTO THIN STRIPS ACROSS

THE GRAIN

1 MEDIUM ONION, SLICED THINLY

2 CLOVES GARLIC, CRUSHED

SALT AND PEPPER

SAUCE:

2 TEASPOONS CORNFLOUR

4 TABLESPOONS WATER

3 TABLESPOONS SOY SAUCE

FINELY GRATED RIND AND JUICE OF ½ LEMON

2 TABLESPOONS RICE WINE OR DRY SHERRY

First prepare the sauce: mix the cornflour to a thin paste with the water, then stir in the soy sauce, lemon rind and juice and the rice wine or sherry. Set aside.

Blanch the beans in boiling salted water for 2 minutes. Drain, rinse immediately under cold running water and drain again. Set aside.

Heat the wok until hot. Add 1 tablespoon of the oil and heat over a moderate heat until hot. Add the pine kernels and stir-fry for about 30 seconds or until toasted. Remove the wok from the heat and transfer the pine kernels to kitchen paper with a slotted spoon. Leave to drain.

Return the wok to the heat. Add the chicken strips, increase the heat to high and stir-fry for 3-4 minutes or until lightly coloured on all sides. Remove the wok from the heat and transfer the chicken to a plate with a slotted spoon. Set aside.

Return the wok to a moderate heat, add the remaining oil and heat until hot. Add the sliced onion and garlic and stir-fry for 1-2 minutes or until softened, taking care not to let them brown.

Stir the sauce to mix, then pour into the wok. Increase the heat to high and stir for 30 seconds, then add the green beans and the chicken and its juices. Toss for 1-2 minutes or until all the ingredients are combined and piping hot, then stir in the pine kernels. Add pepper to taste and serve at once.

Serves 3-4 as a main dish with accompaniments, or as part of an oriental meal

PINE KERNELS

PINE KERNELS COME FROM THE STONE PINE TREE, *PINUS PINEA*, WHICH GROWS IN MANY PARTS OF THE WORLD, BUT PARTICULARLY AROUND THE MEDITERRANEAN. THE OUTER CASING IS VERY HARD, AND ONLY THE KERNEL FROM INSIDE IS SOLD COMMERCIALLY. ALTHOUGH MOSTLY ASSOCIATED WITH MEDITERRANEAN DISHES, PARTICULARLY THE ITALIAN PESTO SAUCE, PINE KERNELS ARE GOOD IN STIR-FRIES BECAUSE OF THEIR APPEALING, DAINTY SHAPE. THEY HAVE A DISTINCTIVE FLAVOUR AND CREAMY TEXTURE, AND GO PARTICULARLY WELL WITH POULTRY. THEY ARE ALSO GOOD IN VEGETARIAN STIR-FRIES, BECAUSE THEY ARE RICH IN PROTEIN. TO INCREASE THEIR NUTTY FLAVOUR, YOU CAN DRY-FRY OR TOAST THEM BEFORE ADDING TO A STIR-FRY, SHAKING THE PAN CONSTANTLY AS THEY TEND TO BURN EASILY.

SHANGHAI CHICKEN

2 TABLESPOONS VEGETABLE OIL

40 G (1½ OZ) PINE KERNELS

4 SKINNED AND BONED CHICKEN BREASTS, EACH WEIGHING
ABOUT 150 G (5 OZ), CUT INTO THIN STRIPS ACROSS
THE GRAIN

1 LARGE RED PEPPER, CORED, SEEDED AND CUT LENGTHWAYS
INTO THIN STRIPS

2.5 CM (1 INCH) PIECE FRESH ROOT GINGER, PEELED AND
CHOPPED FINELY

250 G (8 OZ) CHINESE LEAVES, SHREDDED

250 G (8 OZ) BEAN SPROUTS

4 SPRING ONIONS, SLICED THINLY ON THE DIAGONAL

1-2 TEASPOONS SESAME OIL

SAUCE:

2 TEASPOONS CORNFLOUR

6 TABLESPOONS COLD CHICKEN STOCK OR WATER

3 TABLESPOONS SOY SAUCE

2 TABLESPOONS RICE WINE OR DRY SHERRY

1½ TABLESPOONS SOFT BROWN SUGAR

First prepare the sauce: mix the cornflour to a thin paste with the stock or water, then stir in the soy sauce, rice wine or sherry and sugar.

Heat the wok until hot. Add 1 tablespoon of the oil and heat over a moderate heat until hot. Add the pine kernels and stir-fry for 1-2 minutes or until toasted. Remove the wok from the heat and transfer the pine kernels to kitchen paper with a slotted spoon. Leave to drain.

Return the wok to the heat, add the remaining oil and heat until hot. Add the chicken strips, increase the heat to high and stir-fry for 3-4 minutes or until lightly coloured on all sides. Remove the wok from the heat and transfer the chicken to a plate with a slotted spoon. Set aside.

Return the wok to a moderate heat. Add the red pepper and ginger and stir-fry for 2-3 minutes or until the pepper is just beginning to soften. Add the Chinese leaves, bean sprouts and spring onions and stir-fry for a further minute.

Stir the sauce to mix, then pour into the wok and bring to the boil over a moderate heat, stirring constantly. Return the chicken and its juices to the wok, increase the heat to high and toss for 1-2 minutes or until all the ingredients are combined and piping hot. Serve at once, sprinkled with the toasted pine kernels and the sesame oil.

Serves 3-4 as a main dish with accompaniments, or as part of an oriental meal

FIVE-SPICE CHICKEN

Five-spice powder is available from the spice racks of supermarkets, and in oriental stores. A combination of five ground spices – anise, cinnamon, cloves, fennel and Szechuan peppercorns – it is used in both Chinese and Malaysian cooking. Aromatic rather than hot and spicy, it goes well with the delicate flavour of chicken.

3 TABLESPOONS VEGETABLE OIL

4 SKINNED AND BONED CHICKEN BREASTS, EACH WEIGHING
ABOUT 150 G (5 OZ), CUT INTO THIN STRIPS ACROSS
THE GRAIN

1 MEDIUM ONION, SLICED THINLY

3 MEDIUM CARROTS, CUT INTO JULIENNE STRIPS

125 G (4 OZ) CAULIFLOWER FLORETS, DIVIDED INTO
TINY SPRIGS

1½ TEASPOONS FIVE-SPICE POWDER

75 ML (3 FL OZ) CHICKEN STOCK OR WATER

2 TABLESPOONS SOY SAUCE

1 X 227 G (7½ OZ) CAN WATER CHESTNUTS, DRAINED
AND SLICED

PEPPER

Heat the wok until hot. Add the oil and heat over a moderate heat until hot. Add the chicken strips, increase the heat to high and stir-fry for 3-4 minutes or until lightly coloured on all sides. Remove the wok from the heat and transfer the chicken to a plate with a slotted spoon. Set aside.

Add the onion, carrots and cauliflower to the wok and sprinkle over the five-spice powder. Stir-fry for 3-4 minutes or until softened, taking care not to let the ingredients brown. Add the stock or water and soy sauce and stir until bubbling.

Return the chicken and its juices to the wok and add the water chestnuts. Toss for 1-2 minutes or until all the ingredients are combined and piping hot. Add pepper to taste and serve at once.

Serves 3-4 as a main dish with accompaniments, or 4 as part of an oriental meal

CHICKEN WITH RICE AND MIXED VEGETABLES

This tasty 'all-in-one' dish makes a good midweek supper.
Serve it with a crisp green or colourful mixed salad.

175 G (6 OZ) LONG-GRAIN RICE

600 ML (1 PINT) CHICKEN STOCK

2 TEASPOONS TURMERIC

2 TABLESPOONS VEGETABLE OIL

4 RASHERS SMOKED STREAKY BACON, RINDED AND CUT INTO THIN STRIPS

1 SMALL ONION, CHOPPED FINELY

3 CELERY STICKS, CHOPPED FINELY

4 SKINNED AND BONED CHICKEN BREASTS, EACH WEIGHING ABOUT 150 G (5 OZ), DICED

75 G (3 OZ) FROZEN PEAS

50 G (2 OZ) FROZEN SWEETCORN KERNELS

4 RIPE TOMATOES, SKINNED AND CHOPPED ROUGHLY

SALT AND PEPPER

DRESSING:

4 TABLESPOONS OLIVE OIL

1 TABLESPOON LEMON JUICE OR CIDER VINEGAR

ABOUT 4 TABLESPOONS CHOPPED FRESH CORIANDER

Put the rice in a medium saucepan. Add the chicken stock and turmeric and bring to the boil. Stir once, cover with a lid and simmer for 15 minutes, or until the stock is just absorbed by the rice.

Meanwhile, prepare the dressing: whisk the olive oil in a jug or bowl with the lemon juice or cider vinegar, the coriander and salt and pepper to taste. Set aside.

Heat the wok until hot. Add 1 tablespoon of the oil and heat over a moderate heat until hot. Add the bacon strips and stir-fry until crisp. Remove with a slotted spoon and drain on kitchen paper.

Heat the remaining oil in the wok, add the onion and celery and stir-fry for 2-3 minutes or until softened, taking care not to let them brown. Add the chicken, increase the heat to high and stir-fry for 3-4 minutes or until lightly coloured.

Add the peas, sweetcorn and tomatoes and toss to combine with the chicken. Stir-fry for a further 2-3 minutes, then add the rice and toss to combine with all the ingredients in the wok. Pour over the dressing and toss until heated through. Taste for seasoning and then serve hot, sprinkled with the crispy bacon.

Serves 4 as a supper dish, with salad as an accompaniment

SHREDDED TURKEY WITH MIXED VEGETABLES

After soaking the dried mushrooms, don't throw the soaking
liquid away, but add it to the sauce ingredients for
extra flavour.

75 G (3 OZ) FLAKED ALMONDS

4 TABLESPOONS VEGETABLE OIL

500 G (1 LB) TURKEY BREAST FILLETS, CUT INTO THIN STRIPS ACROSS THE GRAIN

3 MEDIUM CARROTS, SLICED THINLY ON THE DIAGONAL

5-15 G (¼-½ OZ) DRIED SHIITAKE MUSHROOMS, SOAKED IN WARM WATER FOR 20 MINUTES, DRAINED AND CHOPPED

375 G (12 OZ) BROCCOLI FLORETS, TRIMMED AND DIVIDED INTO SMALL SPRIGS

½ BUNCH SPRING ONIONS, SLICED THINLY ON THE DIAGONAL

2 TEASPOONS SESAME OIL

PEPPER

SAUCE:

2 TEASPOONS CORNFLOUR

6 TABLESPOONS WATER

4 TABLESPOONS SOY SAUCE

4 TABLESPOONS RICE WINE OR DRY SHERRY

First prepare the sauce: mix the cornflour to a thin paste with the water, then stir in the soy sauce and rice wine or sherry. Set aside.

Heat the wok until hot. Add the almonds and dry-fry over a gentle heat until golden brown. Remove and set aside.

Add 2 tablespoons of the vegetable oil to the wok and heat over a moderate heat until hot. Add the turkey strips, increase the heat to high and stir-fry for 3-4 minutes or until lightly coloured on all sides. Remove the wok from the heat and tip the turkey and its juices into a bowl. Set aside.

Return the wok to a moderate heat, add the remaining oil and heat until hot. Add the carrots, dried mushrooms and broccoli stalks and stir-fry for 3-4 minutes. Add the broccoli florets and spring onions and stir-fry for a further 30 seconds.

Stir the sauce to mix, then pour into the wok. Increase the heat to high and stir until the sauce thickens, then return the turkey and its juices to the wok and toss for 1-2 minutes or until all the ingredients are combined and piping hot. Add pepper to taste and serve at once, sprinkled with the sesame oil and toasted almonds.

Serves 3-4 as a main dish with accompaniments, or as part of an oriental meal

MUSAMAN CHICKEN CURRY

100 G (3½ OZ) CREAMED COCONUT, CHOPPED ROUGHLY

1 MEDIUM ONION, CHOPPED ROUGHLY

2 CLOVES GARLIC, CHOPPED ROUGHLY

5 CM (2 INCH) PIECE FRESH ROOT GINGER, PEELED AND
CHOPPED FINELY

2 DRIED RED CHILLIES, CHOPPED FINELY

GRATED RIND AND JUICE OF 1 LIME

50 G (2 OZ) SHELLED PEANUTS (NATURAL ROASTED),
CHOPPED ROUGHLY

2 TEASPOONS CORIANDER SEEDS

SEEDS OF 6 CARDAMOM PODS

1 X 227 G (7½ OZ) CAN PINEAPPLE CHUNKS IN
NATURAL JUICE

4 TABLESPOONS CHOPPED FRESH BASIL

2 TEASPOONS ANCHOVY ESSENCE

1 TEASPOON TURMERIC

2 TABLESPOONS VEGETABLE OIL

8 BONELESS CHICKEN THIGHS, SKINNED AND CUT INTO
LARGE CHUNKS

SALT AND PEPPER

First make the coconut milk: put the chopped coconut in a measuring jug, pour in boiling water up to the 300 ml (½ pint) mark and stir until the coconut is dissolved. Set aside.

Put the onion in a food processor with the garlic, ginger, chillies, lime rind and juice, peanuts, coriander and cardamom seeds. Add the juice from the pineapple and work to a paste. Add the paste to the coconut milk with half of the basil, the anchovy essence, turmeric and a pinch of salt. Stir well to mix and set aside.

Heat the wok until hot. Add the oil and heat over a moderate heat until hot. Add the chicken, increase the heat to high and stir-fry for 1-2 minutes or until the chicken is lightly coloured on all sides. Add the coconut milk mixture and bring to the boil, stirring constantly.

Lower the heat and simmer for about 10 minutes or until the chicken is tender and the sauce thickened, stirring frequently to prevent sticking. Add the chunks of pineapple and heat through, then taste for seasoning. Serve hot, sprinkled with the remaining basil.

Serves 4 as a main dish, with accompaniments

FRESH PINEAPPLE

IN THAILAND AND OTHER TROPICAL COUNTRIES OF THE FAR EAST, FRESH PINEAPPLE IS FREQUENTLY INCLUDED IN SAVOURY DISHES, PARTICULARLY WITH MEAT AND POULTRY. IMPORTED PINEAPPLES ARE AT THEIR CHEAPEST AND BEST HERE IN THE SPRING, AND ARE WELL WORTH BUYING TO GIVE A FRESH FRUITY FLAVOUR TO STIR-FRIES, AND TO ADD VITAMIN C.

TO TEST A FRESH PINEAPPLE FOR RIPENESS, PULL A LEAF AWAY FROM THE PLUME OR CROWN — IT SHOULD COME AWAY EASILY. A GOOD, JUICY PINEAPPLE WILL WEIGH HEAVY, AND HAVE A SWEET, HEADY AROMA.

TO CUT A FRESH PINEAPPLE INTO CHUNKS: CUT OFF THE PLUME OR CROWN AND A SLICE FROM THE BASE; STAND THE PINEAPPLE UPRIGHT ON A BOARD AND, HOLDING THE FRUIT FIRMLY WITH ONE HAND, CUT THE SKIN AWAY IN STRIPS, WORKING FROM THE TOP OF THE FRUIT TO THE BOTTOM AND CUTTING DEEP ENOUGH TO REMOVE THE EYES WITH THE SKIN. CUT THE FLESH AWAY FROM THE HARD CENTRAL CORE IN STRIPS, THEN SLICE THESE CROSSWAYS INTO BITE-SIZED CHUNKS.

BANG BANG CHICKEN

4 SKINNED AND BONED CHICKEN BREASTS, EACH WEIGHING

ABOUT 150 G (5 OZ)

6 TABLESPOONS SOY SAUCE

2 TABLESPOONS SESAME OIL

2.5 CM (1 INCH) PIECE FRESH ROOT GINGER, CHOPPED FINELY

2 TABLESPOONS SESAME SEEDS

4 TABLESPOONS VEGETABLE OIL

4 SMALL CARROTS, CUT INTO JULIENNE STRIPS

1 FRESH GREEN OR RED CHILLI, SEEDED AND CHOPPED

125 G (4 OZ) BEAN SPROUTS

½ CUCUMBER, CUT INTO JULIENNE STRIPS

3 TABLESPOONS RICE WINE OR DRY SHERRY

2 TABLESPOONS CLEAR HONEY

150 ML (¼ PINT) CHICKEN STOCK

FLAT LEAF PARSLEY TO GARNISH

Place the chicken between 2 sheets of greaseproof paper and bang hard with a rolling pin to flatten and tenderize them. Cut the chicken into thin strips across the grain, then place in a shallow dish. Mix 2 tablespoons of the soy sauce with the sesame oil and ginger. Pour over the chicken and turn to coat. Cover and leave to stand for 20 minutes, turning occasionally.

Meanwhile, heat the wok until hot. Add the sesame seeds and dry-fry over a gentle heat for 1-2 minutes or until toasted, tossing them so they do not catch and burn. Remove the wok from the heat and tip the seeds on to a plate. Set aside.

Return the wok to a moderate heat, add 2 tablespoons of the vegetable oil and heat until hot. Add the carrots and chilli and stir-fry for 2-3 minutes. Remove with a slotted spoon and place in a bowl. Add the bean sprouts to the wok and stir-fry for 1 minute, then remove the wok from the heat and tip the bean sprouts into the bowl. Add the cucumber and toss well.

Return the wok to the heat, add the remaining oil and heat until hot. Add the chicken, increase the heat and stir-fry for 4-5 minutes. Remove the wok from the heat and transfer the chicken to a separate bowl with a slotted spoon.

Return the wok to the heat, add the remaining soy sauce, the rice wine or sherry, honey and stock. Bring to the boil, stirring, then simmer for a few minutes, stirring constantly, until reduced slightly. Pour half of the sauce mixture over the vegetables and half over the chicken. Stir to mix. Cover and leave to cool, stirring occasionally.

Arrange the chicken and vegetables together on individual plates, drizzle over any sauce remaining in the bowls and sprinkle with the sesame seeds. Garnish with parsley and serve.

Serves 4 as a starter or light lunch

A WARM SALAD OF TURKEY AND WILD MUSHROOMS

2 HEADS SMALL, CRISP LETTUCE, LEAVES SEPARATED

3 TABLESPOONS OLIVE OIL

2-3 RASHERS SMOKED BACON, RINDED AND CUT INTO

THIN STRIPS

500 G (1 LB) TURKEY BREAST FILLETS, CUT INTO THIN STRIPS

ACROSS THE GRAIN

125 G (4 OZ) FRESH WILD MUSHROOMS, LEFT WHOLE OR

SLICED THINLY IF LARGE

JUICE OF 1 LEMON

SALT AND PEPPER

DRESSING:

4 TABLESPOONS OLIVE OIL

2 TABLESPOONS WINE VINEGAR (RED OR WHITE)

1 CLOVE GARLIC, CRUSHED

¼ TEASPOON COARSE GRAIN OR DIJON MUSTARD

PINCH OF SUGAR

First prepare the dressing: put all the ingredients in a jug and whisk to combine. Set aside.

Put the lettuce leaves in a large salad bowl, tearing them into bite-sized pieces if you like.

Heat the wok until hot. Add 1 tablespoon of the oil and heat over a moderate heat until hot. Add the bacon and stir-fry for 3-4 minutes or until crisp. Remove the wok from the heat and transfer the bacon to kitchen paper with a slotted spoon. Leave to drain.

Return the wok to the heat, add another 1 tablespoon of the oil and heat until hot. Add the turkey strips, increase the heat to high and stir-fry for 3-4 minutes or until lightly coloured on all sides. Remove the wok from the heat and tip the turkey and its juices into a bowl. Keep hot.

Return the wok to a moderate heat, add the remaining oil and heat until hot. Add the mushrooms, lemon juice and salt and pepper to taste, increase the heat to high and stir-fry until all the liquid has evaporated. Tip the contents of the wok into the bowl with the turkey and toss to combine.

Pour the dressing into the wok and stir until hot and sizzling. Quickly add the turkey and mushroom mixture to the bowl of lettuce, pour over the sizzling dressing and toss quickly to combine. Taste for seasoning and serve at once, sprinkled with the crispy bacon.

Serves 4 as a light supper or lunch dish

SESAME CHICKEN

*This dish is simple and quick. Serve it with a colourful,
crunchy mixed vegetable stir-fry.*

2 EGG WHITES

2 TABLESPOONS CORNFLOUR

2 TABLESPOONS SESAME SEEDS

¼ TEASPOON SALT

4 SKINNED AND BONED CHICKEN BREASTS, EACH WEIGHING
ABOUT 150 G (5 OZ), CUT INTO THIN STRIPS ACROSS
THE GRAIN

ABOUT 300 ML (½ PINT) VEGETABLE OIL FOR
SHALLOW-FRYING

2 TEASPOONS SESAME OIL

SAUCE:

2 TABLESPOONS SOY SAUCE

2 TABLESPOONS RICE WINE OR DRY SHERRY

1 TABLESPOON WINE VINEGAR (RED OR WHITE)

2 TEASPOONS SOFT BROWN SUGAR

½ TEASPOON CHILLI POWDER, OR TO TASTE

First prepare the sauce: mix all the ingredients together in a
jug or bowl. Set aside.

Lightly beat the egg whites in a shallow dish with the
cornflour, sesame seeds and salt. Add the strips of chicken and
turn to coat. Set aside.

Heat the oil in the wok until hot but not smoking. One at a
time, lift the strips of chicken out of the egg white mixture
with a fork and drop into the hot oil. Shallow-fry the chicken
in batches for about 3-4 minutes at a time until golden. Lift
out with a slotted spoon and drain on kitchen paper. Keep hot
in the oven while shallow-frying the remainder.

Pour off all the oil from the wok and wipe clean with
kitchen paper. Return the wok to a moderate heat, pour in the
sauce and stir until sizzling. Return the chicken to the wok
and toss for 1-2 minutes or until evenly coated in the sauce.
Sprinkle over the sesame oil and serve at once.

Serves 3-4 as a main dish with accompaniments, or as part of
an oriental meal

STRANGE-FLAVOURED CHICKEN

*This oddly named Chinese dish is not strangely flavoured at
all – it is absolutely delicious! Very hot and spicy, it
combines the flavour of sesame with soy, ginger, garlic and
chilli. Plain boiled rice is the essential accompaniment to act
as a foil to the strong flavours. Sesame paste is sold as
'tahini' in health food shops and Greek and Cypriot stores.*

2 TABLESPOONS SESAME SEEDS

2 TABLESPOONS VEGETABLE OIL

2 TABLESPOONS FINELY CHOPPED SPRING ONIONS

2.5 CM (1 INCH) PIECE FRESH ROOT GINGER, PEELED AND
CHOPPED VERY FINELY

1 CLOVE GARLIC, CRUSHED

4 SKINNED AND BONED CHICKEN BREASTS, EACH WEIGHING
ABOUT 150 G (5 OZ), CUT INTO STRIPS ACROSS THE GRAIN

2 TABLESPOONS SESAME PASTE (TAHINI)

2 TABLESPOONS SOY SAUCE

2 TABLESPOONS CHILLI SAUCE

1 TABLESPOON WATER

2 TEASPOONS SESAME OIL

Heat the wok until hot. Add the sesame seeds and dry-fry over
a gentle heat until toasted. Tip the sesame seeds out of the
wok and set aside.

Add the oil to the wok, increase the heat to moderate and
heat until the oil is hot. Add the spring onions, ginger and
garlic and stir-fry for 30 seconds. Add the chicken strips,
increase the heat to high and stir-fry for 3-4 minutes or until
lightly coloured on all sides.

Add the sesame paste, soy and chilli sauces and the water
and toss for 1-2 minutes or until all the ingredients are
combined and piping hot. Sprinkle over the sesame oil and
toasted sesame seeds. Serve at once.

Serves 3-4 as a main dish with accompaniments, or as part of
an oriental meal

SPICY MARINATED CHICKEN

Don't leave the chicken any longer than 2 hours in the marinade, or the coating will harden on the chicken strips. Avoid marinating in the refrigerator, as again it will make the coating hard.

1 SMALL ONION, CHOPPED ROUGHLY

2.5 CM (1 INCH) PIECE FRESH ROOT GINGER, PEELED AND CHOPPED ROUGHLY

1 CLOVE GARLIC, CHOPPED ROUGHLY

50 G (2 OZ) CREAMED COCONUT, CHOPPED ROUGHLY

2 TEASPOONS GROUND CORIANDER

2 TEASPOONS TURMERIC

SEEDS OF 2 CARDAMOM PODS

½ TEASPOON SALT

4 TABLESPOONS HOT WATER

8 BONELESS CHICKEN THIGHS, SKINNED AND CUT INTO STRIPS

2 EGGS, BEATEN

ABOUT 300 ML (½ PINT) VEGETABLE OIL FOR SHALLOW-FRYING

LEMON OR LIME WEDGES TO SERVE

Put the onion, ginger, garlic and coconut in a food processor with the spices, salt and hot water. Work to a paste, then remove from the food processor and turn into a bowl. Add the chicken, cover and leave to marinate for 1-2 hours in a cool place (not the refrigerator), turning the chicken occasionally.

Place a batch of the marinated chicken strips in the beaten eggs and turn to coat. Heat the oil in the wok until hot but not smoking. With a fork, lift the strips of chicken out of the eggs one at a time and immediately drop into the hot oil. Shallow-fry the chicken in batches for about 3-4 minutes at a time until golden, then lift out with a draining spoon and place on kitchen paper to drain. Keep hot in the oven while shallow-frying the remainder. Serve the chicken hot, with lemon or lime wedges.

Serves 3-4 as a main dish with accompaniments, or as part of an oriental meal

SZECHUAN CHICKEN WITH WALNUTS

Ingredients for stir-fries should all be of a similar size and shape, so try to cut the chicken, spring onions and green pepper into dice the same size as the walnut pieces.

1 EGG WHITE

1 TABLESPOON CORNFLOUR

4 SKINNED AND BONED CHICKEN BREASTS, EACH WEIGHING ABOUT 150 G (5 OZ), DICED

2 TABLESPOONS VEGETABLE OIL

½ BUNCH SPRING ONIONS, CHOPPED

1 LARGE GREEN PEPPER, CORED, SEEDED AND DICED

2 FRESH CHILLIES, SEEDED AND CHOPPED FINELY

50 G (2 OZ) WALNUT PIECES

SAUCE:

2 TEASPOONS CORNFLOUR

4 TABLESPOONS WATER

2 TABLESPOONS YELLOW BEAN SAUCE

2 TABLESPOONS RICE WINE OR DRY SHERRY

1 TEASPOON SOFT BROWN SUGAR

First prepare the sauce: mix the cornflour to a thin paste with the water, then stir in the yellow bean sauce, rice wine or sherry and sugar. Set aside.

Mix the egg white and cornflour together in a shallow dish, add the diced chicken and turn to coat.

Heat the wok until hot. Add the oil and heat over a moderate heat until hot. Add the chicken, increase the heat to high and stir-fry for 3-4 minutes or until lightly coloured on all sides. Remove the wok from the heat and transfer the chicken to a bowl with a slotted spoon. Set aside.

Return the wok to a moderate heat, add the spring onions, green pepper and chillies and stir-fry for 2-3 minutes or until softened slightly, taking care not to let the ingredients brown.

Stir the sauce to mix, pour into the wok and increase the heat to high. Return the chicken to the wok and toss for 1-2 minutes or until all the ingredients are combined and piping hot. Add the walnuts and toss for 30 seconds longer. Serve at once.

Serves 3-4 as a main dish with accompaniments, or as part of an oriental meal

LAMB & PORK

BOTH LAMB AND PORK ARE USED IN ORIENTAL COOKING, ALTHOUGH PORK IS A FAVOURITE WITH CHINESE COOKS. LEAN, TENDER CUTS SUITABLE FOR STIR-FRYING ARE AVAILABLE PRE-PACKAGED AT SUPERMARKETS. THESE ARE SOLD READY-TRIMMED WITH VIRTUALLY NO WASTE, A SAVING IN TIME AND MONEY.

ORANGE GLAZED PORK

THINLY PARED RIND OF **1** LARGE ORANGE, CUT INTO
MATCHSTICK STRIPS

3 TABLESPOONS VEGETABLE OIL

500 G (1 LB) PORK FILLET (TENDERLOIN), SLICED THINLY
ACROSS THE GRAIN

1 MEDIUM ONION, CHOPPED FINELY

2.5 CM (1 INCH) PIECE FRESH ROOT GINGER, PEELED AND
CHOPPED FINELY

4 TABLESPOONS ORANGE JUICE

4 TABLESPOONS CLEAR HONEY

2 TABLESPOONS CRUNCHY PEANUT BUTTER

2 TABLESPOONS SOY SAUCE

½ TEASPOON CHILLI POWDER, OR MORE TO TASTE

MINT SPRIGS TO GARNISH

Blanch the strips of orange rind in boiling water for 1 minute. Drain, rinse under cold water and drain again. Set aside.

Heat the wok until hot. Add 2 tablespoons of the oil and heat over a moderate heat until hot. Add the pork strips, increase the heat to high and stir-fry for 3-4 minutes or until lightly coloured on all sides. Remove the wok from the heat and tip the pork and its juices into a bowl. Set aside.

Return the wok to a moderate heat, add the remaining oil and heat until hot. Add the onion and ginger and stir-fry for 2-3 minutes or until softened, taking care not to let the ingredients brown. Stir in the remaining ingredients, bring to the boil and stir for 1 minute.

Return the pork and its juices to the wok, add half of the orange rind and mix well. Toss until all the ingredients are combined and the pork is piping hot. Serve at once, sprinkled with the remaining orange rind and mint sprigs.

Serves 3-4 as a main dish, with noodles as an accompaniment

LAMB WITH OKRA AND TOMATOES

250 G (8 OZ) SMALL OKRA, ENDS OF STALKS REMOVED

3 TABLESPOONS VEGETABLE OIL

1 MEDIUM ONION, SLICED THINLY

1-2 CLOVES GARLIC, CRUSHED

2 TEASPOONS GROUND CORIANDER

2 TEASPOONS TURMERIC

1 TEASPOON HOT CHILLI POWDER, OR TO TASTE

500 G (1 LB) LAMB FILLET, CUT INTO THIN STRIPS ACROSS
THE GRAIN

250 G (8 OZ) RIPE TOMATOES, SKINNED AND
CHOPPED ROUGHLY

FINELY GRATED RIND AND JUICE OF ½ LEMON

½ TEASPOON CASTER SUGAR

SALT

Blanch the okra in boiling salted water for 5 minutes, then drain, rinse under cold running water and then drain again, Set aside.

Heat the wok until hot. Add the oil and heat over a moderate heat until hot. Add the onion, garlic and spices and stir-fry for 2-3 minutes or until the onion is softened, taking care not to let the ingredients brown.

Add the lamb strips, increase the heat to high and stir-fry for 3-4 minutes or until the lamb is browned on all sides.

Add the tomatoes and stir-fry until the juices run, then add the lemon rind and juice, sugar and salt to taste. Stir-fry to mix, then add the okra and toss for 3-4 minutes or until heated through. Serve hot.

Serves 3-4 as a main dish, with boiled rice as an accompaniment

STIR-FRIED PORK WITH BEAN CURD AND MANGETOUT

250-300 G (8-10 OZ) FIRM BEAN CURD (TOFU)

3 TABLESPOONS VEGETABLE OIL

375 G (12 OZ) PORK FILLET (TENDERLOIN), CUT INTO THIN STRIPS ACROSS THE GRAIN

125 G (4 OZ) MANGETOUT, TOPS REMOVED

2 CLOVES GARLIC, CRUSHED

250 G (8 OZ) CHINESE LEAVES, SHREDDED

1 TEASPOON SESAME OIL

PEPPER

SAUCE:

2 TEASPOONS CORNFLOUR

6 TABLESPOONS COLD CHICKEN STOCK OR WATER

3 TABLESPOONS SOY SAUCE

2 TABLESPOONS RICE WINE OR DRY SHERRY

½ TEASPOON FIVE-SPICE POWDER

½ TEASPOON CHILLI POWDER, OR TO TASTE

First prepare the sauce: mix the cornflour to a paste with 2 tablespoons of the stock or water, then stir in the remaining stock or water and the remaining ingredients. Set aside.

Drain the bean curd, pat dry and cut into cubes.

Heat the wok until hot. Add 2 tablespoons of the vegetable oil and heat over a moderate heat until hot. Add the pork strips, increase the heat to high and stir-fry for 3-4 minutes or until lightly coloured on all sides. Remove the wok from the heat and tip the pork and its juices into a bowl. Set aside.

Return the wok to a moderate heat. Add the remaining vegetable oil and heat until hot. Add the bean curd and stir-fry for 1-2 minutes or until lightly coloured on all sides. Remove the wok from the heat and transfer the bean curd to kitchen paper with a slotted spoon. Keep hot.

Return the wok to the heat and add the mangetout and garlic. Stir-fry for 2 minutes. Return the pork and its juices to the wok, add the Chinese leaves and stir-fry for 30 seconds, just until mixed with the pork and mangetout.

Stir the sauce to mix, then pour into the wok. Increase the heat to high and stir for 1-2 minutes or until the sauce thickens. Gently fold in the bean curd. Add pepper to taste and sprinkle with the sesame oil. Serve at once.

Serves 3-4 as a main dish with accompaniments, or as part of an oriental meal

PEKING PORK

The flavourings in this simple stir-fry are typical of northern Chinese cooking. As vegetables are not included, serve a mixed vegetable dish and rice or noodles on the side.

2 TABLESPOONS VEGETABLE OIL

4 SPRING ONIONS, SLICED THINLY ON THE DIAGONAL

5 CM (2 INCH) PIECE FRESH ROOT GINGER, PEELED AND CHOPPED FINELY

2 CLOVES GARLIC, CRUSHED

500 G (1 LB) PORK FILLET (TENDERLOIN), CUT INTO THIN STRIPS ACROSS THE GRAIN

2 TEASPOONS SESAME OIL

PEPPER

SAUCE:

2 TEASPOONS CORNFLOUR

4 TABLESPOONS WATER

3 TABLESPOONS RICE WINE OR DRY SHERRY

3 TABLESPOONS SOY SAUCE

1 TEASPOON SOFT BROWN SUGAR

First prepare the sauce: mix the cornflour to a thin paste with the water, then stir in the remaining ingredients. Set aside.

Heat the wok until hot. Add the oil and heat over a moderate heat until hot. Add the spring onions, ginger and garlic and stir-fry for 30 seconds to flavour the oil. Remove with a slotted spoon and drain on kitchen paper.

Add the pork strips to the wok, increase the heat to high and stir-fry for 3-4 minutes or until the pork is lightly coloured on all sides.

Stir the sauce to mix, pour into the wok and stir for 1 minute. Return the spring onion mixture to the wok and toss until all the ingredients are well combined and piping hot. Add pepper to taste, sprinkle over the sesame oil and serve at once.

Serves 3-4 as a main dish, with accompaniments

SZECHUAN KIDNEYS

8 LAMBS' KIDNEYS

½ TEASPOON BICARBONATE OF SODA

1 TEASPOON CIDER VINEGAR

½ TEASPOON SALT

1 TEASPOON SZECHUAN PEPPERCORNS

2 TABLESPOONS VEGETABLE OIL

2.5 CM (1 INCH) PIECE FRESH ROOT GINGER, PEELED AND

CHOPPED FINELY

4 SPRING ONIONS, CHOPPED FINELY

2 CLOVES GARLIC, CHOPPED FINELY

½ TEASPOON HOT CHILLI POWDER, OR MORE

ACCORDING TO TASTE

SAUCE:

2 TEASPOONS CORNFLOUR

4 TABLESPOONS WATER

2 TABLESPOONS SOY SAUCE

2 TABLESPOONS RICE WINE OR DRY SHERRY

½ TEASPOON SOFT BROWN SUGAR

Remove any membrane from around the kidneys, then cut each kidney in half lengthways. Cut out and discard the cores from the centres and discard any fat. With a sharp knife, score the outer surface of each kidney half in a criss-cross pattern, then cut the kidneys into small pieces. Place the kidneys in a bowl, sprinkle over the bicarbonate of soda and turn to coat. Leave to stand for about 20 minutes.

Rinse the kidneys under cold running water, then return them to the bowl and add the cider vinegar and salt. Turn to coat, then transfer them to a sieve and leave them to drain for about 30 minutes.

Meanwhile, prepare the sauce ingredients: mix the cornflour to a thin paste with the water, then stir in the soy sauce, rice wine or sherry and sugar. Set aside.

Heat the wok until hot. Add the Szechuan peppercorns and dry-fry for 2-3 minutes. Tip out the peppercorns, then crush in a mortar and pestle. Set aside.

Pat the kidneys dry with kitchen paper. Heat the wok until hot. Add the oil and heat over a moderate heat until hot. Add the kidneys and stir-fry for about 1 minute, then add the ginger, spring onions, garlic, crushed Szechuan pepper and chilli powder and stir-fry for 2-3 minutes longer.

Stir the sauce to mix, pour into the wok and stir for 1-2 minutes or until bubbling. Serve hot.

Serves 2-3 as a main dish, with accompaniments

SWEET AND SOUR PORK WITH PINEAPPLE

2 TABLESPOONS SOY SAUCE

1 TABLESPOON CORNFLOUR

500 G (1 LB) PORK FILLET (TENDERLOIN), CUT INTO

BITE-SIZED CUBES

1 TABLESPOON VEGETABLE OIL

1 SMALL RED PEPPER, CORED, SEEDED AND CUT LENGTHWAYS

INTO THIN STRIPS

1 SMALL GREEN PEPPER, CORED, SEEDED AND CUT

LENGTHWAYS INTO THIN STRIPS

ABOUT 600 ML (1 PINT) VEGETABLE OIL, FOR DEEP-FRYING

1 EGG, BEATEN

SAUCE:

2 TEASPOONS CORNFLOUR

2 TABLESPOONS WATER

1 X 227 G (7½ OZ) CAN PINEAPPLE SLICES IN NATURAL

JUICE, DRAINED AND CUT INTO BITE-SIZED CHUNKS, WITH

JUICE RESERVED

2 TABLESPOONS RICE WINE OR DRY SHERRY

2 TABLESPOONS DARK SOFT BROWN SUGAR

2 TABLESPOONS SOY SAUCE

1 TABLESPOON TOMATO KETCHUP

First prepare the sauce: mix the cornflour to a paste with the water, then stir in the pineapple juice, rice wine or sherry, sugar, soy sauce and tomato ketchup. Set aside.

Mix the soy sauce and cornflour together in a shallow dish, add the cubes of pork and stir to mix. Set aside.

Heat the oil in a saucepan over a moderate heat until hot. Add the pepper strips and stir-fry for 2-3 minutes or until just softened. Stir the sauce to mix, then pour into the pan and stir until thickened. Stir in the pieces of pineapple, cover and remove from the heat. Pour the oil for deep-frying into the wok and heat to 180°C-190°C, 350°F-375°F, or until a cube of bread browns in 30 seconds.

Add the beaten egg to the pork and stir to coat. One at a time, lower the cubes of pork into the hot oil with a slotted spoon. Deep-fry in batches for 3-4 minutes or until golden and crisp. Lift out with the slotted spoon and drain on kitchen paper. Keep hot while deep-frying the remainder.

Quickly reheat the sauce until bubbling. Place the cubes of pork in a serving dish and pour over the sauce. Serve at once.

Serves 3-4 as a main dish with accompaniments, or as part of an oriental meal

STIR-FRIED PORK WITH BEAN SPROUTS AND CORN

500 G (1 LB) PORK FILLET (TENDERLOIN), CUT INTO THIN

STRIPS ACROSS THE GRAIN

125 G (4 OZ) BABY CORN

1 TABLESPOON CORNFLOUR

150 ML (¼ PINT) COLD CHICKEN STOCK

2 TABLESPOONS HOISIN SAUCE

3 TABLESPOONS VEGETABLE OIL

½ BUNCH SPRING ONIONS, SLICED THINLY ON THE DIAGONAL

1 MEDIUM RED PEPPER, CORED, SEEDED AND CUT

LENGTHWAYS INTO THIN STRIPS

150 G (5 OZ) BEAN SPROUTS

PEPPER

MARINADE:

2 TABLESPOONS SOY SAUCE

2 TABLESPOONS VEGETABLE OIL

1 TABLESPOON CIDER VINEGAR

1 CLOVE GARLIC, CRUSHED

½ TEASPOON FIVE-SPICE POWDER

First make the marinade: put all the marinade ingredients in a shallow dish and stir well to mix. Add the strips of pork and turn to coat. Cover and leave to marinate for 1-2 hours, turning the pork occasionally.

Meanwhile, blanch the baby corn in boiling water for 2 minutes. Drain, rinse under cold running water and then drain again.

Mix the cornflour to a thin paste with a few spoonfuls of the stock, then stir in the remaining stock and the hoisin sauce.

Heat the wok until hot. Add 2 tablespoons of the oil and heat over a moderate heat until hot. Add the spring onions and red pepper and stir-fry for 2-3 minutes or until softened, taking care not to let the ingredients brown. Add the bean sprouts, increase the heat to high and stir-fry for 1 minute only. Remove the wok from the heat and tip the vegetables into a bowl. Set aside.

Return the wok to a moderate heat. Add the remaining oil and heat until hot. Add the pork and its marinade, increase the heat to high and stir-fry for 3-4 minutes or until lightly coloured on all sides. Stir the stock mixture, pour over the pork and stir until thickened, then add the vegetables and toss until all the ingredients are combined and piping hot. Add pepper to taste and serve at once.

Serves 4 as a main dish, with accompaniments

PORK WITH CUCUMBER

The secret of this tasty dish is not to overcook the cucumber. It should be tender, but still crisp, with a bright green colour.

1 MEDIUM CUCUMBER

2 TABLESPOONS VEGETABLE OIL

½ BUNCH SPRING ONIONS, SLICED THINLY ON THE DIAGONAL

2.5 CM (1 INCH) PIECE FRESH ROOT GINGER, PEELED AND

CHOPPED VERY FINELY

500 G (1 LB) PORK FILLET (TENDERLOIN), CUT INTO THIN

STRIPS ACROSS THE GRAIN

PEPPER

CHOPPED CHIVES TO GARNISH

SAUCE:

1 TABLESPOON CORNFLOUR

150 ML (¼ PINT) COLD CHICKEN STOCK OR WATER

3 TABLESPOONS SOY SAUCE

2 TABLESPOONS RICE WINE OR DRY SHERRY

First prepare the sauce ingredients: mix the cornflour to a paste with 2 tablespoons of the stock or water, then stir in the remaining stock or water, the soy sauce and rice wine or sherry. Set aside.

Cut the cucumber into strips: cut off the ends of the cucumber, then cut the cucumber crossways into 6 equal pieces. Cut each piece of cucumber lengthways into quarters, then cut off the seeds and discard them.

Heat the wok until hot. Add the oil and heat over a moderate heat until hot. Add the spring onions and ginger and stir-fry for a few seconds, then add the pork strips, increase the heat to high and stir-fry for 3-4 minutes or until lightly coloured on all sides.

Stir the sauce to mix, then pour into the wok. Toss until all the ingredients are combined. Add the strips of cucumber and stir for 1-2 minutes or until hot. Add pepper to taste and serve at once, sprinkled with chopped chives.

Serves 3-4 as a main dish with accompaniments, or as part of an oriental meal

LAMB WITH LEEKS

This is a classic Chinese combination, with a sweet and sour sauce. It is made with very few ingredients and it is quick and easy to do.

3 TABLESPOONS VEGETABLE OIL

500 G (1 LB) LAMB FILLET, SLICED THINLY ACROSS
THE GRAIN

4 LEEKS, CUT ON THE DIAGONAL INTO
4 CM (1½ INCH) LENGTHS

2 CLOVES GARLIC, CRUSHED

PEPPER

SAUCE:

2 TEASPOONS CORNFLOUR

4 TABLESPOONS WATER

2 TABLESPOONS SOY SAUCE

2 TEASPOONS RED WINE VINEGAR

2 TEASPOONS CLEAR HONEY

First prepare the sauce: mix the cornflour to a thin paste with the water, then stir in the soy sauce, wine vinegar and honey. Set the sauce aside.

Heat the wok until hot. Add the oil and heat over a moderate heat until hot. Add the lamb, increase the heat to high and stir-fry for 3-4 minutes or until browned on all sides.

Add the leeks and garlic and stir-fry for 2-3 minutes further or until the leeks are just tender. Stir the sauce to mix, then pour into the wok and toss until all the ingredients are combined. Add pepper to taste and serve at once.

Serves 3-4 as a main dish with accompaniments, or as part of an oriental meal

LAMB WITH SPRING ONIONS AND GARLIC

This classic combination is simple and quick to make, yet it is a favourite with everyone.

2 TABLESPOONS VEGETABLE OIL

500 G (1 LB) LAMB FILLET, SLICED THINLY ACROSS
THE GRAIN

2 TABLESPOONS SOY SAUCE

2 TABLESPOONS RICE WINE OR DRY SHERRY

1 TEASPOON CHILLI POWDER

1 TEASPOON DARK SOFT BROWN SUGAR

1 BUNCH SPRING ONIONS, SLICED THINLY ON THE DIAGONAL

3 CLOVES GARLIC, CHOPPED FINELY

Heat the wok until hot. Add the oil and heat over a moderate heat until hot. Add the lamb slices, increase the heat to high and stir-fry for 3-4 minutes or until browned on all sides. Sprinkle over the soy sauce, rice wine or sherry, chilli powder and sugar and stir-fry for 1-2 minutes further.

Add the spring onions and garlic and stir-fry for 30 seconds to mix with the lamb. Serve at once.

Serves 3-4 as a main dish with accompaniments, or as part of an oriental meal

BRAISED PORK BALLS WITH SPICY SAUCE

Serve these tasty pork balls with Chinese egg noodles and a crunchy, colourful vegetable stir-fry.

375 G (12 OZ) PORK FILLET (TENDERLOIN), MINCED

1 EGG WHITE, LIGHTLY BEATEN

1 TEASPOON GROUND GINGER

1 TEASPOON TURMERIC

1 TEASPOON CHILLI POWDER

2 TABLESPOONS VEGETABLE OIL

1 SMALL ONION, CHOPPED FINELY

150 ML (¼ PINT) CHICKEN STOCK OR WATER

1 TABLESPOON TOMATO PURÉE

SALT AND PEPPER

RAW OR FRIED ONION RINGS (SEE PAGE 69) TO GARNISH (OPTIONAL)

Put the minced pork in a bowl, add the egg white, half of the spices, and salt and pepper to taste. Mix with the hands until evenly combined. Shape into 16 balls, then chill in the refrigerator for about 30 minutes.

Heat the wok until hot. Add the oil and heat over a moderate heat until hot. Add half of the pork balls and stir-fry for 3-4 minutes or until browned on all sides. Remove the wok from the heat and transfer the balls to kitchen paper with a slotted spoon. Set aside to drain. Stir-fry the remaining balls in the same way.

Pour off all but 1 tablespoon oil from the wok. Return the wok to a moderate heat, add the onion and stir-fry for 2-3 minutes or until softened. Add the remaining spices and stir-fry for 1-2 minutes, then stir in the stock or water and the tomato purée. Add salt and pepper to taste, then bring to the boil, stirring all the time.

Return the pork balls to the wok and shake to coat in the sauce. Lower the heat, cover the wok and braise gently for 15-20 minutes, or until the balls are cooked through, shaking the wok frequently. Taste the sauce for seasoning. Serve hot, garnished with onion rings if you like.

Serves 4 as a main dish, with accompaniments

LAMB FILLET

LEAN, TENDER MEAT IS BEST FOR STIR-FRYING BECAUSE OF THE VERY SHORT COOKING TIME, BUT A LITTLE FAT MARBLED THROUGHOUT THE MEAT HELPS KEEP IT MOIST. FILLET END OF LEG IS THE OBVIOUS CUT OF LAMB TO CHOOSE, BECAUSE IT IS SO VERY LEAN, BUT IT DOES TEND TO BE RATHER DRY. THE BEST CUT FOR STIR-FRYING IS LAMB FILLET - THE STRIP OF TENDER, BONELESS MEAT TAKEN FROM THE NECK OF THE ANIMAL. AVAILABLE PREPACKED FROM SUPERMARKETS, AND FROM BUTCHERS, IT IS FAR LESS EXPENSIVE THAN LEG, AND A LOT TASTIER TOO, BUT AS THERE IS SUCH A SMALL AMOUNT ON EACH ANIMAL IT IS OFTEN IN SHORT SUPPLY. IF YOU EVER SEE LAMB FILLET, IT IS WELL WORTH BUYING SOME AND FREEZING IT FOR FUTURE USE.

LAMB IN LETTUCE PARCELS

2 TABLESPOONS VEGETABLE OIL

½ BUNCH SPRING ONIONS, SLICED THINLY ON THE DIAGONAL

1 GREEN CHILLI, SEEDED AND CHOPPED FINELY

2 CLOVES GARLIC, CRUSHED

250 G (8 OZ) LAMB FILLET, CUT INTO THIN STRIPS ACROSS THE GRAIN

5-15 G (¼-½ OZ) DRIED SHIITAKE MUSHROOMS, SOAKED IN WARM WATER FOR 20 MINUTES, DRAINED AND CHOPPED ROUGHLY

75 G (3 OZ) BEAN SPROUTS

3 TABLESPOONS SOY SAUCE

PEPPER

ABOUT 4 TABLESPOONS HOISIN SAUCE

8 CRISP LETTUCE LEAVES

FRESH MINT OR BASIL LEAVES

DIPPING SAUCE:

125 ML (4 FL OZ) SOY SAUCE

2 CLOVES GARLIC, CRUSHED

1 TEASPOON CASTER SUGAR

1 TEASPOON LEMON JUICE

First make the dipping sauce: beat all the ingredients together in a small bowl. Set aside.

Heat the wok until hot. Add the oil and heat over a moderate heat until hot. Add the spring onions, chilli and garlic and stir-fry for 2-3 minutes to flavour the oil. Remove the wok from the heat and transfer the flavourings to kitchen paper with a slotted spoon. Set aside to drain.

Return the wok to the heat, add the lamb and increase the heat to high. Stir-fry for 3-4 minutes or until browned on all sides. Add the dried mushrooms and bean sprouts and stir-fry for 2-3 minutes, then return the spring onion mixture to the wok and add the soy sauce. Stir-fry until all the ingredients are evenly combined, then add pepper to taste. Turn off the heat under the wok.

Spoon a little hoisin sauce on to each lettuce leaf, place a few mint or basil leaves on top, then a spoonful of the lamb mixture. Roll up the lettuce around the lamb, tucking the ends in. Serve at once, with the dipping sauce handed separately.

Serves 4 as a starter, or as part of an oriental meal

RAPID-FRIED PORK WITH PEAS

This dish is quite pungent in flavour. A mixture of long-grain and wild rice would make a good accompaniment, to offset the richness of the pork and sauce.

3 TABLESPOONS OLIVE OIL

500 G (1 LB) PORK FILLET (TENDERLOIN), CUT INTO THIN STRIPS ACROSS THE GRAIN

1 MEDIUM ONION, CHOPPED FINELY

2 CLOVES GARLIC, CRUSHED

125 ML (4 FL OZ) RED WINE

1 TABLESPOON RED WINE VINEGAR

1 TABLESPOON TOMATO PURÉE

½ TEASPOON CAYENNE PEPPER

¼ TEASPOON CASTER SUGAR

250 G (8 OZ) FROZEN PEAS

2 TABLESPOONS CHOPPED FRESH CORIANDER

SALT AND PEPPER

CORIANDER SPRIGS TO GARNISH

Heat the wok until hot. Add 2 tablespoons of the oil and heat over a moderate heat until hot. Add the pork, increase the heat to high and stir-fry for 3-4 minutes or until lightly coloured on all sides. Remove the wok from the heat and tip the pork and its juices into a bowl. Set aside.

Return the wok to a moderate heat. Add the remaining oil and heat until hot. Add the onion and garlic and stir-fry for 2-3 minutes or until softened, taking care not to let the ingredients brown. Stir in the wine, wine vinegar, tomato purée, cayenne and sugar. Bring to the boil, stirring, then add the peas and salt and pepper to taste. Simmer for 5 minutes or until the peas are tender.

Return the pork and its juices to the wok, increase the heat to high and toss until all the ingredients are combined and the pork is piping hot. Remove the wok from the heat, stir in the chopped coriander and taste for seasoning. Serve at once, garnished with coriander sprigs.

Serves 4 as a main dish, with rice as an accompaniment

HONEYED PORK

2 TABLESPOONS VEGETABLE OIL

2 TABLESPOONS FLAKED ALMONDS

500 G (1 LB) PORK FILLET (TENDERLOIN), CUT INTO THIN
STRIPS ACROSS THE GRAIN

SAUCE:

2 TEASPOONS CORNFLOUR

4 TABLESPOONS WATER

2 TABLESPOONS CLEAR HONEY

1 TABLESPOON SOY SAUCE

1 TABLESPOON RICE WINE OR DRY SHERRY

1 TEASPOON FIVE-SPICE POWDER

First prepare the sauce ingredients: mix the cornflour to a thin paste with the water, then stir in the honey, soy sauce, rice wine or sherry and five-spice powder. Set aside.

Heat the wok until hot. Add the oil and heat over a moderate heat until hot. Add the almonds and stir-fry for 2-3 minutes or until golden brown, then remove with a slotted spoon and drain on kitchen paper.

Add the pork strips to the wok, increase the heat to high and stir-fry for 3-4 minutes or until lightly coloured on all sides. Stir the sauce to mix and pour into the wok, then stir for 1-2 minutes further, or until the pork is coated with the sauce. Serve at once, sprinkled with the almonds.

Serves 4 as a main dish, with accompaniments

SPICED LAMB WITH SHREDDED SPINACH

If fresh spinach is not in season, you can use frozen whole leaf spinach, but make sure you defrost and drain it very thoroughly before adding it to the lamb or the finished dish will be very watery. If you like spicy hot food, you can dry-fry and crush 1-2 dried red chillies with the spice seeds.

1 TABLESPOON CUMIN SEEDS

1 TABLESPOON CORIANDER SEEDS

1 TEASPOON MUSTARD SEEDS

2 TABLESPOONS VEGETABLE OIL

1 MEDIUM ONION, CHOPPED FINELY

500 G (1 LB) LAMB FILLET, CUT INTO THIN STRIPS ACROSS
THE GRAIN

2 CLOVES GARLIC, CRUSHED

2 TEASPOONS TURMERIC

150 ML (¼ PINT) CHICKEN STOCK OR WATER

175 G (6 OZ) SPINACH, SHREDDED

SALT AND PEPPER

Heat the wok until hot, add the cumin, coriander and mustard seeds and dry-fry over a gentle heat for 2-3 minutes or until their aroma is released. Remove the wok from the heat and crush the seeds in a mortar and pestle.

Return the wok to a moderate heat, add the oil and heat until hot. Add the onion and stir-fry for 2-3 minutes or until softened, taking care not to let it brown. Add the lamb strips, garlic, crushed spices and the turmeric. Increase the heat to high and stir-fry for 3-4 minutes or until the lamb is browned on all sides. Add the stock or water and salt and pepper to taste. Stir well to mix, then add the shredded spinach and toss for 30 seconds or just until beginning to wilt. Taste for seasoning and serve at once.

Serves 4 as a main dish, with accompaniments

LAMB WITH SPICY HOT SAUCE

Take care! This simple stir-fry is fiery hot.

3 TABLESPOONS VEGETABLE OIL

500 G (1 LB) LAMB FILLET, CUT INTO THIN STRIPS ACROSS THE GRAIN

4 SPRING ONIONS, SLICED THINLY ON THE DIAGONAL

2 CLOVES GARLIC, CRUSHED

SAUCE:

2 TEASPOONS CORNFLOUR

4 TABLESPOONS WATER

2 TABLESPOONS HOT CHILLI SAUCE

1 TABLESPOON WINE VINEGAR (RED OR WHITE)

2 TEASPOONS DARK SOFT BROWN SUGAR

½ TEASPOON FIVE-SPICE POWDER

First prepare the sauce: mix the cornflour to a thin paste with the water, then stir in the chilli sauce, wine vinegar, sugar and five-spice powder. Set aside.

Heat the wok until hot. Add 2 tablespoons of the oil and heat over a moderate heat until hot. Add the lamb strips, increase the heat to high and stir-fry for 3-4 minutes or until browned on all sides. Remove the wok from the heat and tip the lamb and its juices into a bowl. Set aside.

Return the wok to a moderate heat. Add the remaining oil and heat until hot. Add the spring onions and garlic and stir-fry for 30 seconds. Remove with a slotted spoon and set aside.

Stir the sauce to mix, pour into the wok and increase the heat to high. Stir until the sauce thickens, then add the lamb and its juices and the spring onion mixture. Toss for 1-2 minutes or until piping hot. Serve at once.

Serves 3-4 as a main dish with accompaniments, or as part of an oriental meal

FRIED ONION RINGS

ONIONS, DEEP-FRIED UNTIL CRISP, ARE A POPULAR ACCOMPANIMENT TO MANY ORIENTAL DISHES. THEY CAN BE SERVED AT THE TABLE IN A SMALL BOWL TO BE HANDED ROUND SEPARATELY, OR THEY CAN BE SPRINKLED OVER FOOD AS A GARNISH.

SLICE 1 LARGE ONION INTO THIN RINGS. HEAT ABOUT 300 ML (½ PINT) VEGETABLE OIL IN A WOK OR DEEP-FAT FRYER UNTIL HOT BUT NOT SMOKING. ADD THE ONION RINGS AND DEEP-FRY UNTIL GOLDEN BROWN, ABOUT 3-4 MINUTES DEPENDING ON THE TEMPERATURE OF THE OIL. REMOVE WITH A SLOTTED SPOON AND DRAIN ON KITCHEN PAPER. SERVE HOT OR AT ROOM TEMPERATURE.

ORIENTAL LAMB

This simple stir-fry is full of crisp, crunchy and colourful vegetables, which make the lamb nutritious and fresh-tasting. You can ring the changes with different vegetables according to the season – there are no hard-and-fast rules. Water chestnuts are available in cans from large supermarkets; they do not have much flavour, but are wonderfully crisp.

3 TABLESPOONS VEGETABLE OIL

500 G (1 LB) LAMB FILLET, CUT INTO THIN STRIPS ACROSS THE GRAIN

3 SPRING ONIONS, SLICED THINLY ON THE DIAGONAL

1 CLOVE GARLIC, CRUSHED

1 SMALL RED PEPPER, CORED, SEEDED AND CUT LENGTHWAYS INTO THIN STRIPS

1 SMALL YELLOW PEPPER, CORED, SEEDED AND CUT LENGTHWAYS INTO THIN STRIPS

2 MEDIUM COURGETTES, SLICED THINLY ON THE DIAGONAL

1 x 227 G (7½ OZ) CAN WATER CHESTNUTS, DRAINED AND SLICED THINLY

PEPPER

SAUCE:

2 TEASPOONS CORNFLOUR

4 TABLESPOONS WATER

2 TABLESPOONS SOY SAUCE

First prepare the sauce ingredients: mix the cornflour to a thin paste with the water, then stir in the soy sauce. Set aside.

Heat the wok until hot. Add 2 tablespoons of the oil and heat over a moderate heat until hot. Add the lamb strips, increase the heat to high and stir-fry for 3-4 minutes or until browned on all sides. Remove the wok from the heat and tip the lamb and its juices into a bowl. Set aside.

Return the wok to a moderate heat, add the remaining oil and heat until hot. Add the spring onions, garlic and peppers and stir-fry for 3-4 minutes. Add the courgettes and stir-fry for a further 2 minutes.

Return the lamb and its juices to the wok, then add the water chestnuts. Stir the sauce to mix, pour into the wok and increase the heat to high. Toss for 2-3 minutes or until all the ingredients are combined and the lamb is piping hot. Add pepper to taste and serve at once.

Serves 4 as a main dish with accompaniments, or as part of an oriental meal

SHREDDED LAMB WITH CRUNCHY VEGETABLES IN YELLOW BEAN SAUCE

You can buy ready-prepared yellow bean sauce in bottles from large supermarkets with oriental sections as well as in oriental stores. Made from crushed yellow beans, vinegar, spices and salt, it adds an instant 'Chinese' flavour to stir-fries, and goes particularly well with lamb.

125 G (4 OZ) BABY CORN

2 MEDIUM CARROTS, SLICED THINLY ON THE DIAGONAL

125 G (4 OZ) GREEN BEANS, CUT INTO 4 CM (1½ INCH) LENGTHS, OR MANGETOUT, TOPS REMOVED

3 TABLESPOONS VEGETABLE OIL

500 G (1 LB) LAMB FILLET, SHREDDED ACROSS THE GRAIN

4 SPRING ONIONS, SLICED THINLY ON THE DIAGONAL

2.5 CM (1 INCH) PIECE FRESH ROOT GINGER, PEELED AND SHREDDED FINELY

1 CLOVE GARLIC, CHOPPED FINELY

1 x 227 G (7½ OZ) CAN SLICED BAMBOO SHOOTS, DRAINED

1 x 160 G (5½ OZ) BOTTLE STIR-FRY YELLOW BEAN SAUCE

SALT AND PEPPER

Blanch the baby corn, carrots and green beans or mangetout in boiling salted water for 2 minutes. Drain and set aside.

Heat the wok until hot. Add 2 tablespoons of the oil and heat over a moderate heat until hot. Add the lamb, increase the heat to high and stir-fry for about 3-4 minutes or until browned on all sides. Remove the wok from the heat and tip the lamb and its juices into a bowl. Set aside.

Return the wok to a moderate heat and heat the remaining oil until hot. Add the spring onions, ginger and garlic and stir-fry for 30 seconds to flavour the oil. Add the blanched vegetables, increase the heat to high and stir-fry for about 2 minutes or until heated through.

Return the lamb with its juices to the wok, add the bamboo shoots and stir in the yellow bean sauce. Bring to the boil and stir-fry for 3-4 minures or until piping hot. Add salt and pepper to taste and serve at once.

Serves 3-4 as a main dish with accompaniments, or as part of an oriental meal

MALAY LAMB WITH HOT CHILLI SAUCE

In this recipe, terasi, a kind of concentrated shrimp paste, is used to give a pungent 'fishy' aroma and flavour, which goes especially well with lamb and is typically South-East Asian. Terasi can be bought in oriental stores, where it is sometimes also called blachan or kapi. If you cannot obtain it, use anchovy essence or pounded canned anchovies instead.

2 TABLESPOONS VEGETABLE OIL

500 G (1 LB) LAMB FILLET, CUT INTO BITE-SIZED CHUNKS

1 CM (½ INCH) PIECE TERASI

3 TABLESPOONS CRUNCHY PEANUT BUTTER

½ TEASPOON HOT CHILLI POWDER

6 TABLESPOONS WATER

MARINADE:

3 TABLESPOONS SOY SAUCE

2 TABLESPOONS LEMON JUICE

1 SMALL ONION, CHOPPED FINELY

2 CLOVES GARLIC, CRUSHED

2.5 CM (1 INCH) PIECE FRESH ROOT GINGER, PEELED AND CHOPPED FINELY

1 TEASPOON GROUND CORIANDER

1 TEASPOON SOFT BROWN SUGAR

½ TEASPOON HOT CHILLI POWDER

First make the marinade: put all the marinade ingredients in a shallow dish and stir well to mix. Add the lamb and turn to coat. Cover and leave in the refrigerator for at least 4 hours, turning the lamb occasionally.

Heat the wok until hot. Add the oil and heat over a moderate heat until hot. Add the lamb, increase the heat to high and stir-fry for 3-4 minutes or until browned on all sides. Remove the wok from the heat and tip the lamb and its juices into a bowl. Set aside.

Pound the terasi and mix with the peanut butter and chilli powder. Return the wok to a moderate heat and add the terasi mixture with any remaining marinade and the water. Stir for a few minutes until bubbling, making sure the terasi is thoroughly cooked. Return the lamb and its juices to the wok, increase the heat to high and toss until all the ingredients are combined. Serve hot.

Serves 3-4 as a main dish with accompaniments, or as part of an oriental meal

LAMB WITH WALNUTS

This is a classic Chinese stir-fry, quick and easy to make, and very delicious. Take care not to cook the walnuts longer than the time given in the recipe or they will discolour the sauce and make the whole dish look unattractive.

½ X 160 G (5½ OZ) BOTTLE YELLOW BEAN SAUCE

2 TABLESPOONS RICE WINE OR DRY SHERRY

2 TABLESPOONS WATER

2 TABLESPOONS VEGETABLE OIL

500 G (1 LB) LAMB FILLET, CUT INTO THIN STRIPS ACROSS THE GRAIN

2 CLOVES GARLIC, CRUSHED

½ BUNCH SPRING ONIONS, SLICED THINLY ON THE DIAGONAL

50 G (2 OZ) WALNUT PIECES

SALT AND PEPPER

First mix the yellow bean sauce with the rice wine or sherry and the water. Set aside.

Heat the wok until hot. Add the oil and heat over a moderate heat until hot. Add the lamb and garlic, increase the heat to high and stir-fry for 3-4 minutes or until the lamb is browned on all sides.

Add the spring onions and stir-fry for 1 minute, then add the yellow bean sauce mixture and stir-fry for 1 minute longer. Add the walnuts and toss for 30 seconds just until heated through. Add salt and pepper to taste and serve at once.

Serves 3-4 as a main dish with accompaniments, or as part of an oriental meal

HOT AND SPICY PORK

500 G (1 LB) PORK FILLET (TENDERLOIN), SLICED THINLY

ACROSS THE GRAIN

3 TABLESPOONS SOY SAUCE

2 TABLESPOONS CIDER VINEGAR

2 TEASPOONS CORNFLOUR

2.5 CM (1 INCH) PIECE FRESH ROOT GINGER, PEELED AND

CHOPPED ROUGHLY

1 CLOVE GARLIC, CHOPPED ROUGHLY

2 DRIED RED CHILLIES, CHOPPED ROUGHLY

4 TABLESPOONS VEGETABLE OIL

1 LARGE RED PEPPER, CORED, SEEDED AND CUT LENGTHWAYS

INTO THIN STRIPS

250 G (8 OZ) MANGETOUT, TOPS REMOVED

250 G (8 OZ) FIRM BEAN CURD (TOFU), DRAINED AND CUBED

125 ML (4 FL OZ) CHICKEN STOCK, MADE FROM A CUBE

1-2 TABLESPOONS CHILLI SAUCE, ACCORDING TO TASTE

PEPPER

Place the pork slices in a bowl, add the soy sauce, cider vinegar and cornflour and stir well to mix. Set aside.

Pound the ginger, garlic and chillies in a mortar and pestle.

Heat the wok until hot. Add 1 tablespoon of the oil and heat over a moderate heat until hot. Add the red pepper and mangetout, sprinkle with pepper to taste and stir-fry for 3 minutes. Remove the wok from the heat and transfer the vegetables to a plate with a slotted spoon. Set aside.

Return the wok to a moderate heat, add 2 tablespoons of the oil and heat until hot. Add the bean curd and stir-fry gently for 1-2 minutes or until lightly coloured, taking care not to break it up. Remove the wok from the heat and transfer the bean curd to kitchen paper with a slotted spoon. Keep hot.

Return the wok to a moderate heat, add the remaining oil and heat until hot. Add the pounded mixture and stir-fry for 2-3 minutes, taking care not to let the ingredients brown. Add the pork, increase the heat to high and stir-fry for 3-4 minutes or until lightly coloured on all sides. Remove the wok from the heat and transfer the pork to a plate with a slotted spoon. Set aside.

Pour the stock into the wok and bring to the boil, stirring, then stir in the chilli sauce. Return the pork and its juices to the wok with the red pepper and mangetout. Increase the heat to high and toss until all the ingredients are combined. Gently stir in the bean curd and serve at once.

Serves 4 as a main dish, with accompaniments

SPRING ONION TASSELS

SPRING ONIONS ARE A FAVOURITE ORIENTAL VEGETABLE, USED FREQUENTLY BOTH AS AN INGREDIENT IN STIR-FRIES AND AS AN ATTRACTIVE, FRESH AND CRUNCHY GARNISH. ONE OF THE PRETTIEST WAYS TO USE THEM AS A GARNISH IS IN THE FORM OF 'TASSELS' OR 'BRUSHES' AS THEY ARE SOMETIMES ALSO CALLED. TRIM OFF THE ROOTS OF THE SPRING ONIONS, KEEPING THE ENDS INTACT. CUT THE STEMS TO ABOUT 5-7.5 CM (2-3 INCHES) LONG, THEN MAKE SEVERAL LENGTHWAYS CUTS IN EACH STEM, CUTTING JUST TO THE ROOT BUT WITHOUT CUTTING THROUGH IT. DROP THE SPRING ONIONS INTO A BOWL OF ICED WATER AND PLACE IN THE REFRIGERATOR. LEAVE TO CHILL FOR AT LEAST 30 MINUTES, UNTIL THE ENDS CURL UP AND OPEN OUT. DRAIN WELL BEFORE USE.

BEEF

Rich, juicy beef is at its most succulent in stir-fries, and with today's leaner cuts you can keep fat and cholesterol down. In this chapter you will find delicious combinations of beef with colourful, crunchy vegetables and sauces that are full of exotic flavour.

BEEF WITH PINEAPPLE

500 G (1 LB) RUMP OR FILLET STEAK, CUT INTO THIN STRIPS

2 TEASPOONS CORNFLOUR

4 TABLESPOONS COLD BEEF STOCK OR WATER

2 TABLESPOONS RICE WINE OR DRY SHERRY

2 TEASPOONS DARK SOFT BROWN SUGAR

3 TABLESPOONS VEGETABLE OIL

3 CELERY STICKS, SLICED THINLY ON THE DIAGONAL

4 SLICES FRESH PINEAPPLE, CUBED

SALT AND PEPPER

MARINADE:

2.5 CM (1 INCH) PIECE FRESH ROOT GINGER, CHOPPED FINELY

2 TABLESPOONS VEGETABLE OIL

2 TABLESPOONS SOY SAUCE

1 TABLESPOON RED WINE VINEGAR

¼ TEASPOON FIVE-SPICE POWDER

Make the marinade: put all the ingredients in a dish, add the beef and turn to coat. Cover and marinate for 30 minutes, turning the beef occasionally.

Mix the cornflour to a thin paste with the stock or water, then stir in the rice wine or sherry and the sugar. Set aside.

Heat the wok until hot. Add 2 tablespoons of the oil and heat until hot. Add the beef and marinade, increase the heat and stir-fry for 3-4 minutes. Remove the wok from the heat and tip the beef and its juices into a bowl. Set aside.

Return the wok to a moderate heat, add the remaining oil and heat until hot. Add the celery and stir-fry for 2-3 minutes. Stir the cornflour mixture, then pour over the celery and stir to mix. Return the beef to the wok, increase the heat to high and toss until the ingredients are combined. Add the pineapple and toss until heated through. Season to taste and serve.

Serves 3-4 as a main dish with accompaniments

HOT THAI BEEF SALAD

This contrast of fiery hot meat and refreshing, colourful fruits is visually charming – and tantalizing to the tastebuds! Thai food is usually hot and chillies are a favourite ingredient. If you prefer a milder taste, include only a few of the chilli seeds, or none at all.

2 RIPE PAPAYAS, PEELED AND SLICED THINLY

½ LARGE CUCUMBER, CUT THINLY INTO MATCHSTICK STRIPS

75 G (3 OZ) BEAN SPROUTS

1 MEDIUM HEAD CRISP LETTUCE, SHREDDED

2 TABLESPOONS VEGETABLE OIL

500 G (1 LB) RUMP OR FILLET STEAK, CUT INTO THIN STRIPS ACROSS THE GRAIN

3 CLOVES GARLIC, CHOPPED FINELY

2 FRESH GREEN CHILLIES, SLICED INTO THIN RINGS

JUICE OF 2 LEMONS

1 TABLESPOON NAM PLA (FISH SAUCE)

2 TEASPOONS CASTER SUGAR

Arrange the papaya, cucumber, bean sprouts and lettuce in individual piles on a large serving platter. Cover loosely and set aside.

Heat the wok until hot. Add the oil and heat over a moderate heat until hot. Add the beef, garlic and chillies, increase the heat to high and stir-fry for 3-4 minutes or until browned on all sides. Pour in the lemon juice and nam pla, add the sugar and stir-fry until sizzling.

Remove the wok from the heat. Remove the beef from the dressing with a slotted spoon and arrange in the centre of the platter. Drizzle the dressing over the salad ingredients. Serve hot, tossing the ingredients together at the table.

Serves 4 as a light main course

SUKIYAKI BEEF

*This Japanese-inspired dish is given its authentic flavour by
using bottled teriyaki marinade, a type of Japanese soy sauce
mixed with wine and spices. It can be bought at large
supermarkets. Mirin is sweet Japanese rice wine, available at
Japanese and other oriental supermarkets. If you cannot find
it, you can use sweet sherry instead, but the flavour will not
be quite the same. A typical Japanese accompaniment to this
beef dish would be steamed short-grain Japanese rice.
Available at Japanese supermarkets, it has a fragrant aroma
and flavour and is sticky when cooked, making it perfect for
eating with chopsticks.*

5 CM (2 INCH) PIECE FRESH ROOT GINGER, PEELED AND

CHOPPED ROUGHLY

3 CLOVES GARLIC, CHOPPED ROUGHLY

6 BLACK PEPPERCORNS

500 G (1 LB) FILLET STEAK, CUT INTO THIN STRIPS

ACROSS THE GRAIN

6 TABLESPOONS TERIYAKI MARINADE

4 TABLESPOONS MIRIN

2 TABLESPOONS CASTER SUGAR

2 TABLESPOONS VEGETABLE OIL

First pound the ginger, garlic and black peppercorns in a
mortar and pestle.

Place the beef strips in a shallow dish with the pounded
mixture, teriyaki marinade, mirin and sugar. Turn to coat,
then cover and leave to marinate in the refrigerator for
24 hours, turning the beef occasionally.

When ready to cook, let the beef come to room temperature
for about 1 hour.

Heat the wok until hot. Add the oil and heat over a
moderate heat until hot. Remove the beef from the marinade
with a slotted spoon, add to the wok and increase the heat to
high. Stir-fry for 1 minute, then pour over the marinade and
stir-fry for a further minute. Serve at once.

Serves 3-4 as a main dish, with accompaniments

CALVES' LIVER WITH FENNEL AND ORANGE

*Be careful not to overcook calves' liver or it will be tough. It
is a great delicacy and should be treated as such.*

2 TABLESPOONS OLIVE OIL

1 MEDIUM ONION, SLICED THINLY

1 SMALL HEAD FENNEL, WEIGHING 125-150 G (4-5 OZ),

SLICED THINLY

175-250 G (6-8 OZ) CALVES' LIVER, SLICED THINLY

INTO STRIPS

SALT AND PEPPER

SAUCE:

2 TEASPOONS CORNFLOUR

4 TABLESPOONS WATER

4 TABLESPOONS DRY WHITE WINE

FINELY GRATED RIND AND JUICE OF 1 ORANGE

2 TABLESPOONS DRY SHERRY

TO GARNISH:

FENNEL TOPS

ORANGE SLICES

First prepare the sauce: mix the cornflour to a thin paste with
the water, then stir in the white wine, orange rind and juice
and sherry. Set aside.

Heat the wok until hot. Add the oil and heat over a
moderate heat until hot. Add the onion and fennel and stir-
fry for 5 minutes or until softened.

Add the strips of liver and stir-fry for 1-2 minutes or until
browned on all sides.

Stir the sauce to mix, then pour over the liver. Increase the
heat to high and stir for a further 2-3 minutes or until the
sauce is thickened and bubbling.

Add salt and pepper to taste and serve at once, garnished
with fennel tops and orange.

Serves 2 as a main dish, with accompaniments

SIZZLING BEEF

2 TABLESPOONS VEGETABLE OIL

6 SPRING ONIONS, SLICED THINLY ON THE DIAGONAL

4 CELERY STICKS, SLICED THINLY ON THE DIAGONAL

500 G (1 LB) RUMP OR FILLET STEAK, CUT INTO THIN STRIPS
ACROSS THE GRAIN

4 TABLESPOONS BEEF STOCK OR WATER

2 TABLESPOONS SHERRY VINEGAR

2 TEASPOONS WORCESTERSHIRE SAUCE

2 TEASPOONS TOMATO PURÉE

SALT AND PEPPER

Heat the wok until hot. Add the oil and heat over a moderate heat until hot. Add the spring onions and celery and stir-fry for 2-3 minutes or until slightly softened. Add the beef strips, increase the heat to high and stir-fry for 3-4 minutes or until browned on all sides.

Add the stock or water, sherry vinegar, Worcestershire sauce, tomato purée and salt and pepper to taste. Stir-fry until sizzling. Serve at once.

Serves 3-4 as a main dish with accompaniments, or as part of an oriental meal

BEEF WITH BOK CHOY IN OYSTER SAUCE

A classic dish from the Cantonese region of China. Bok choy, sometimes also called 'pak choi' or Chinese cabbage, is excellent in stir-fries. It has a crisp texture, is juicy when bitten into, and has a mild mustard flavour. Take care not to overcook it or you will lose its best qualities. If you are unable to obtain it, Swiss chard can be substituted.

500 G (1 LB) RUMP OR FILLET STEAK, CUT INTO THIN STRIPS
ACROSS THE GRAIN

3 TABLESPOONS VEGETABLE OIL

300 G (10 OZ) BOK CHOY, SHREDDED

5 SPRING ONIONS, SLICED THINLY ON THE DIAGONAL

2.5 CM (1 INCH) PIECE FRESH ROOT GINGER, PEELED AND
CHOPPED FINELY

½ TEASPOON SALT

2 TABLESPOONS OYSTER SAUCE

PEPPER

MARINADE:

2 CLOVES GARLIC, CRUSHED

3 TABLESPOONS SOY SAUCE

2 TABLESPOONS RICE WINE OR DRY SHERRY

1 TEASPOON CASTER SUGAR

First make the marinade: put the garlic in a shallow dish with the soy sauce, rice wine or sherry and sugar. Add the beef strips and turn to coat. Cover and leave to marinate for about 30 minutes, turning the meat occasionally.

Heat the wok until hot. Add 2 tablespoons of the oil and heat over a moderate heat until hot. Add the beef and its marinade, increase the heat to high and stir-fry for 3-4 minutes or until browned on all sides. Remove the wok from the heat and tip the beef and its juices into a bowl. Set aside.

Return the wok to a moderate heat. Add the remaining oil and heat until hot. Add the bok choy, spring onions, ginger and salt and stir-fry for 1-2 minutes or until the bok choy is just starting to wilt.

Return the beef and its juices to the wok, add the oyster sauce and increase the heat to high. Toss until all the ingredients are evenly combined. Add pepper to taste and serve at once.

Serves 3-4 as a main dish with accompaniments, or as part of an oriental meal

HOT SPICED BEEF

This Indonesian-style curry has an interesting cooking method in that the meat and coconut sauce are stir-fried until the oil separates out and the meat becomes coated in a thick, almost dry sauce. Take care when cooking at the end and stir continually, never leaving the wok for a moment or the sauce may catch on the bottom and taste scorched.

150 G (5 OZ) CREAMED COCONUT, CHOPPED ROUGHLY

2 CLOVES GARLIC, CHOPPED ROUGHLY

2.5 CM (1 INCH) PIECE FRESH ROOT GINGER, PEELED AND CHOPPED ROUGHLY

2 DRIED RED CHILLIES, CHOPPED ROUGHLY

2 TABLESPOONS VEGETABLE OIL

1 MEDIUM ONION, CHOPPED FINELY

500 G (1 LB) RUMP STEAK, CUT INTO BITE-SIZED PIECES

1 TEASPOON TURMERIC

1 STEM LEMON GRASS, BRUISED

SALT

TO GARNISH:

BAY LEAVES

LEMON BALM OR BLANCHED SHREDDED LEMON RIND

First make the coconut milk: put the chopped coconut in a measuring jug, pour in boiling water up to the 300 ml (½ pint) mark and stir until the coconut is dissolved. Set aside.

Pound the garlic, ginger and chillies in a mortar and pestle.

Heat the wok until hot. Add the oil and heat over a moderate heat until hot. Add the onion and pounded mixture and stir-fry for 2-3 minutes or until softened, taking care not to let the ingredients brown.

Add the beef, increase the heat to high and stir-fry for 3-4 minutes or until browned on all sides. Pour in the coconut milk and bring to the boil, stirring all the time. Sprinkle in the turmeric and salt to taste and stir to mix. Lower the heat, add the lemon grass and simmer gently for about 20 minutes or until the sauce is thick, stirring frequently to prevent the sauce sticking to the bottom of the wok.

Increase the heat to high and stir for a further 5 minutes, or until the oil separates out from the coconut sauce. Continue stirring until the mixture is quite dry. Remove and discard the lemon grass. Serve hot, garnished with bay leaves, lemon balm or lemon rind.

Serves 4 as a main dish, with accompaniments

SZECHUAN PEPPER BEEF

Szechuan peppercorns, available from spice racks in large supermarkets, are aromatic rather than hot like black or white pepper. They are used extensively in the Szechuan region of China, which is noted for its hot and fiery cuisine. This recipe is typical, combining Szechuan peppercorns with chillies and garlic to create a pungent effect.

1 TABLESPOON SZECHUAN PEPPERCORNS

3 TABLESPOONS VEGETABLE OIL

500 G (1 LB) RUMP OR FILLET STEAK, CUT INTO THIN STRIPS ACROSS THE GRAIN

1 LARGE RED PEPPER, CORED, SEEDED AND CUT LENGTHWAYS INTO THIN STRIPS

2 RED CHILLIES, SEEDED AND CHOPPED FINELY

2.5 CM (1 INCH) PIECE FRESH ROOT GINGER, PEELED AND CUT INTO MATCHSTICK STRIPS

2 CLOVES GARLIC, CRUSHED

SAUCE:

2 TEASPOONS CORNFLOUR

4 TABLESPOONS WATER

3 TABLESPOONS SOY SAUCE

2 TEASPOONS DARK SOFT BROWN SUGAR

First prepare the sauce: mix the cornflour to a thin paste with the water, then stir in the soy sauce and sugar. Set aside.

Heat the wok until hot. Add the Szechuan peppercorns and dry-fry over a gentle heat for 1-2 minutes. Remove from the wok and crush in a mortar and pestle. Set aside.

Add half of the oil to the wok and heat over a moderate heat until hot. Add the beef strips and crushed peppercorns, increase the heat to high and stir-fry for 3-4 minutes or until the beef is browned on all sides. Remove the wok from the heat and tip the beef and its juices into a bowl. Set aside.

Return the wok to a moderate heat. Add the remaining oil and heat until hot. Add the red pepper, chillies, ginger and garlic and stir-fry for 2-3 minutes or until softened, taking care not to let the ingredients brown.

Return the beef and its juices to the wok and stir to mix with the vegetables. Stir the sauce to mix, then pour over the beef and vegetables. Increase the heat to high and toss until the beef is hot and all the ingredients are evenly combined. Serve at once.

Serves 3-4 as a main dish with accompaniments, or as part of an oriental meal

KOREAN BEEF

In Korea, beef stir-fries like this one are often served scooped into lettuce leaves and eaten with the fingers. The cool lettuce and the hot, spicy beef make the most delicious combination. Nam pla (fish sauce) made from fermented fish, is sold in bottles in oriental stores. It is inexpensive and keeps indefinitely, so is well worth buying to add an instant fishy flavour to oriental and other savoury dishes.

500 G (1 LB) RUMP OR FILLET STEAK, CUT INTO THIN STRIPS
ACROSS THE GRAIN

2 CLOVES GARLIC, CRUSHED

4 TABLESPOONS SOY SAUCE

2 TABLESPOONS RICE WINE OR DRY SHERRY

2 TEASPOONS DARK SOFT BROWN SUGAR

PEPPER

2 TEASPOONS SESAME SEEDS

2 TABLESPOONS VEGETABLE OIL

1 LEEK, SHREDDED FINELY

3 MEDIUM CARROTS, CUT INTO MATCHSTICK STRIPS

1 TABLESPOON SESAME OIL

Place the beef strips in a shallow dish with the garlic, soy sauce, rice wine or sherry, sugar and plenty of pepper. Turn to coat, then cover and leave to marinate in the refrigerator for 24 hours, turning the beef occasionally.

When ready to cook, let the beef come to room temperature for about 1 hour. Meanwhile, heat the wok until hot. Place the sesame seeds in the wok and dry-fry over a moderate heat for 1-2 minutes until toasted. Remove from the wok and set aside.

Return the wok to a moderate heat, add the vegetable oil and heat until hot. Add the leek and carrots and stir-fry for 2-3 minutes or until softened. Add the beef and its marinade, increase the heat to high and stir-fry for 3-4 minutes or until browned on all sides. Serve at once, sprinkled with the sesame oil and toasted sesame seeds.

Serves 4 as a main dish, with accompaniments

BRAISED MEATBALLS

375 G (12 OZ) MINCED BEEF

75 G (3 OZ) CREAMED COCONUT, GRATED

2 CLOVES GARLIC, CRUSHED

1 EGG YOLK

4 TEASPOONS SOY SAUCE

300 ML (½ PINT) VEGETABLE OIL FOR SHALLOW-FRYING

1 MEDIUM ONION, SLICED THINLY INTO RINGS

2 CELERY STICKS, SLICED INTO CHUNKY PIECES

3 MEDIUM CARROTS, SLICED INTO RINGS

300 ML (½ PINT) BEEF STOCK

GRATED COCONUT TO GARNISH (OPTIONAL)

Put the minced beef in a bowl, add the grated coconut, the garlic, egg yolk and 2 teaspoons of the soy sauce. Mix well with your hands, then shape into 16 balls. Chill in the refrigerator for about 30 minutes or until firm.

Pour the oil into the wok and heat over a moderate heat until hot but not smoking. shallow-fry the meatballs in batches for 3-4 minutes or until browned on all sides. Lift the meatballs out of the oil with a slotted spoon and drain on kitchen paper.

Pour off all but 2 tablespoons oil from the wok. Add the onion, celery and carrots and stir-fry for 30 seconds. Pour in the stock, add the remaining soy sauce and bring to the boil. Return the meatballs to the wok and baste with the cooking liquid. Cover and braise for 10-15 minutes or until the liquid has reduced and the meatballs are coated in the sauce, shaking the wok frequently and basting from time to time. Serve hot, sprinkled with grated coconut if you like.

Serves 4 as a main dish, with accompaniments

Cantonese Beef with Green Pepper and Black Bean Sauce

This spicy hot, simple beef stir-fry comes from the Canton region of China, where practising Muslims cannot eat pork (the most popular meat for stir-fries in China).

Try to cut the beef and green pepper into the same size squares and the spring onions into pieces the same length as the sides of the squares. This way the finished dish not only looks neat but is also easy to eat with chopsticks.

Black bean sauce is sold in bottles in most large supermarkets with oriental sections.

3 TABLESPOONS VEGETABLE OIL

500 G (1 LB) RUMP OR FILLET STEAK, SLICED THINLY AND CUT INTO SMALL SQUARES

1-2 SMALL DRIED RED CHILLIES, CRUSHED, OR 1-2 TEASPOONS HOT CHILLI POWDER, ACCORDING TO TASTE

1 LARGE GREEN PEPPER, CORED, SEEDED AND SLICED INTO SMALL SQUARES

6 SPRING ONIONS, CUT INTO SHORT LENGTHS

SAUCE:

2 TEASPOONS CORNFLOUR

4 TABLESPOONS WATER

2 TABLESPOONS BLACK BEAN SAUCE

1 TABLESPOON SOY SAUCE

1 TABLESPOON RICE WINE OR DRY SHERRY

1 TEASPOON CASTER SUGAR

First prepare the sauce: mix the cornflour to a thin paste with the water, then stir in the black bean and soy sauces, the rice wine or sherry and the sugar. Set aside.

Heat the wok until hot. Add 2 tablespoons of the oil and heat over a moderate heat until hot. Add the beef and chillies or chilli powder, increase the heat to high and stir-fry for 3-4 minutes or until browned on all sides. Remove the wok from the heat and tip the beef and its juices into a bowl. Set aside.

Return the wok to a moderate heat, add the remaining oil and heat until hot. Add the green pepper and stir-fry for 2-3 minutes or until softened, then add the spring onions. Stir the sauce to mix, then pour into the wok and bring to the boil, stirring.

Return the beef and its juices to the wok, increase the heat to high and toss until coated in the sauce. Serve at once.

Serves 3-4 as a main dish with accompaniments, or as part of an oriental meal

Stir-Fried Beef with Baby Corn and Red Pepper

1 TABLESPOON SZECHUAN PEPPERCORNS

3 TABLESPOONS VEGETABLE OIL

500 G (1 LB) RUMP OR FILLET STEAK, CUT INTO THIN STRIPS ACROSS THE GRAIN

2 FRESH GREEN CHILLIES, SEEDED AND CHOPPED FINELY

1 MEDIUM ONION, SLICED THINLY

1 RED PEPPER, CORED, SEEDED AND CUT LENGTHWAYS INTO THIN STRIPS

1 x 425 G (15 OZ) CAN BABY CORN, DRAINED

SAUCE:

3 TABLESPOONS SOY SAUCE

2 TABLESPOONS RICE WINE OR DRY SHERRY

1 TABLESPOON DARK SOFT BROWN SUGAR

1 TEASPOON FIVE-SPICE POWDER

Heat the wok until hot. Add the Szechuan peppercorns and dry-fry over a gentle heat for 1-2 minutes. Remove from the wok and crush in a mortar and pestle. Set aside.

Prepare the sauce: put all the ingredients in a bowl or jug and stir well to mix. Set aside.

Heat the wok until hot. Add 2 tablespoons of the oil and heat over a moderate heat until hot. Add the beef strips, chillies and crushed Szechuan peppercorns, increase the heat to high and stir-fry for 3-4 minutes or until the beef is browned on all sides. Remove the wok from the heat and tip the beef and its juices into a bowl. Set aside.

Return the wok to a moderate heat, add the remaining oil and heat until hot. Add the onion and red pepper and stir-fry for 2-3 minutes or until softened slightly, then add the baby corn and stir-fry for 1-2 minutes or until hot.

Return the beef and its juices to the wok, pour in the sauce and increase the heat to high. Toss for 2-3 minutes or until all the ingredients are combined and piping hot. Serve at once.

Serves 2-3 as a main dish, or 4 as part of an oriental meal

VEGETABLES

VEGETABLES ARE AT THEIR BEST WHEN COOKED IN THE WOK, BECAUSE STIR-FRYING ALLOWS THEM TO KEEP THEIR NATURAL COLOURS AND CRISP TEXTURE. STIR-FRYING IS ALSO HEALTHY AND QUICK, PERFECT FOR BUSY PEOPLE WHO ARE SHORT OF TIME.

BROCCOLI AND CAULIFLOWER WITH PINE KERNELS

4 TABLESPOONS PINE KERNELS

2 TABLESPOONS VEGETABLE OIL

175 G (6 OZ) BROCCOLI, BROKEN INTO TINY SPRIGS, STALKS CHOPPED

175 G (6 OZ) CAULIFLOWER, BROKEN INTO SPRIGS, STALKS CHOPPED

3 CLOVES GARLIC, CRUSHED

PEPPER

SAUCE:

2 TEASPOONS CORNFLOUR

6 TABLESPOONS COLD VEGETABLE STOCK

2 TABLESPOONS SOY SAUCE

1 TABLESPOON LEMON JUICE

Heat the wok until hot. Add the pine kernels and dry-fry over a gentle heat for 1-2 minutes or until toasted. Remove the wok from the heat and tip out the pine kernels. Set aside.

Prepare the sauce ingredients: mix the cornflour to a paste with 2 tablespoons of the stock, then add the remaining stock, the soy sauce and lemon juice. Set aside.

Return the wok to a moderate heat, add the oil and heat until hot. Add the broccoli and cauliflower stalks, increase the heat to high and stir-fry for 1 minute. Add the sprigs and garlic and stir-fry for a further 2-3 minutes or until tender but still crunchy.

Stir the sauce to mix, pour into the wok and bring to the boil, stirring constantly. Add pepper to taste and serve at once, sprinkled with the toasted pine kernels.

Serves 4 as an accompaniment, or as part of an oriental meal

SHANGHAI STIR-FRY

4 TABLESPOONS BOTTLED SWEET AND SOUR SAUCE

1 x 227 G (8 OZ) CAN PINEAPPLE CHUNKS IN NATURAL JUICE, DRAINED, WITH 3 TABLESPOONS JUICE RESERVED

2 TABLESPOONS VEGETABLE OIL

2 MEDIUM CARROTS, CUT INTO MATCHSTICK STRIPS

1 HEAD FENNEL, SLICED INTO VERY THIN STRIPS, WITH ANY LEAVES RESERVED

1 RED PEPPER, CORED, SEEDED AND CUT LENGTHWAYS INTO THIN STRIPS

1 GREEN PEPPER, CORED, SEEDED AND CUT LENGTHWAYS INTO THIN STRIPS

125 G (4 OZ) BEAN SPROUTS

175 G (6 OZ) CHINESE LEAVES, SHREDDED

SALT AND PEPPER

CHOPPED NUTS (CASHEWS, MACADAMIAS OR PEANUTS) TO GARNISH

First dilute the sweet and sour sauce with the 3 tablespoons reserved pineapple juice. Set aside. Heat the wok until hot. Add the oil and heat over a moderate heat until hot. Add the carrots, fennel and peppers and stir-fry for 3-4 minutes, until just beginning to soften.

Pour the diluted sweet and sour sauce into the wok, increase the heat to high and stir-fry until bubbling. Add the pineapple chunks and bean sprouts and stir-fry for 1 minute or until hot, then add the Chinese leaves and toss for 1 minute further or until all the ingredients are combined and piping hot. Add salt and pepper to taste and serve at once, sprinkled with the chopped nuts and any reserved fennel leaves.

Serves 4-6 as an accompaniment

GREEN BEANS WITH ANCHOVIES AND GARLIC

If you don't want to go to the trouble of draining and crushing canned anchovies, simply buy bottled anchovy essence, which is available at large supermarkets and delicatessens. It is very strong, so you will need only 1-2 teaspoons, according to taste.

1 x 50 G (2 OZ) CAN ANCHOVIES IN OIL, DRAINED

2 TABLESPOONS OLIVE OIL

3 CLOVES GARLIC, CRUSHED

375 G (12 OZ) GREEN BEANS, TOPPED AND TAILED AND CUT IN HALF CROSSWAYS

2-3 TABLESPOONS DRY WHITE WINE

PEPPER

Crush the anchovies with a fork or in a mortar and pestle. Heat the wok until hot. Add the oil and heat over a moderate heat until hot.

Add the crushed anchovies and garlic and stir to mix with the oil, then add the green beans. Increase the heat to high, sprinkle over the wine and stir-fry for 5-6 minutes or until the beans are tender but still crunchy. Add pepper to taste and serve at once.

Serves 4 as an accompaniment

SPINACH WITH BACON AND BUTTON MUSHROOMS

To shred spinach quickly and easily, remove the stalks and any tough ribs from the leaves, then stack several leaves together, one on top of the other. Roll the stack up into a fat cigar shape, then cut crossways into shreds. Repeat with the remaining spinach.

4 RASHERS STREAKY BACON, DERINDED AND CUT INTO STRIPS

1 TABLESPOON OLIVE OIL

250 G (8 OZ) BUTTON MUSHROOMS, SLICED THINLY

2 CLOVES GARLIC, CRUSHED

250 G (8 OZ) FRESH YOUNG SPINACH, SHREDDED

SALT AND PEPPER

6 TABLESPOONS SOURED CREAM TO GARNISH

Heat the wok until hot. Add the bacon and stir-fry over a moderate heat for 3-4 minutes or until crisp. Remove the wok from the heat and transfer the bacon to kitchen paper with a slotted spoon. Leave to drain.

Return the wok to the heat, add the oil and heat until hot. Add the mushrooms, garlic and salt and pepper to taste, increase the heat to high and stir-fry for 1-2 minutes or until the mushrooms are softened. Add the spinach and stir-fry for 30 seconds to 1 minute, or just until it begins to wilt.

Taste and adjust the seasoning if necessary and serve at once, drizzled with the soured cream and sprinkled with the bacon.

Serves 4 as an accompaniment

CARROTS WITH GINGER AND ALMONDS

If you don't have sweet sherry in the house, use dry sherry and a pinch or two of sugar to add a touch of sweetness to the carrots.

50-75 G (2-3 OZ) FLAKED ALMONDS

2 TABLESPOONS VEGETABLE OIL

1 MEDIUM ONION, CHOPPED FINELY

5 CM (2 INCH) PIECE FRESH ROOT GINGER, PEELED AND CUT INTO MATCHSTICK STRIPS

375 G (12 OZ) YOUNG CARROTS, CUT INTO MATCHSTICK STRIPS

4 TABLESPOONS VEGETABLE STOCK OR WATER

2 TABLESPOONS SWEET SHERRY

SALT AND PEPPER

Heat the wok until hot. Add the almonds and dry-fry over a gentle heat until golden brown on all sides. Remove from the wok and set aside.

Add the oil to the wok and heat over a moderate heat until hot. Add the onion and ginger and stir-fry for 2-3 minutes or until softened, taking care not to let them brown.

Add the carrots, stock or water, sherry and salt and pepper to taste. Increase the heat to high and stir-fry for 3-4 minutes or just until the carrots are tender and the liquid has evaporated.

Taste and adjust the seasoning if necessary and serve at once, sprinkled with the toasted almonds.

Serves 4 as an accompaniment

SZECHUAN AUBERGINES

This famous dish is often referred to as 'fish-fragrant aubergine' because it is cooked with the flavourings normally used for fish, namely ginger, garlic and spring onions. The chilli, rice wine, soy sauce, sugar and vinegar add the 'Szechuan' touch. Don't be tempted to skip the salting of the aubergines. This is essential for removing the vegetable's bitter juices.

2 MEDIUM AUBERGINES, TOTAL WEIGHT ABOUT 500 G (1 LB), CUT INTO THIN STRIPS

2 TABLESPOONS VEGETABLE OIL

2.5 CM (1 INCH) PIECE FRESH ROOT GINGER, PEELED AND CHOPPED FINELY

2-3 CLOVES GARLIC, CRUSHED

1 GREEN CHILLI, SEEDED AND CHOPPED VERY FINELY

2 SPRING ONIONS, CHOPPED

2 TABLESPOONS RICE WINE OR DRY SHERRY

1 TABLESPOON SOY SAUCE

1 TEASPOON SUGAR

1 TABLESPOON WHITE WINE OR CIDER VINEGAR

SALT

Place the strips of aubergine in a colander, sprinkling the layers with salt. Cover with a plate, place heavy weights on top and leave to dégorge for 20-30 minutes. Rinse the aubergines well under cold running water, then pat thoroughly dry with a cloth.

Heat the wok until hot. Add the oil and heat over a moderate heat until hot. Add the ginger, garlic, chilli and spring onions and stir-fry for 2-3 minutes or until softened, taking care not to let the ingredients brown.

Add the strips of aubergine and stir-fry for 3-4 minutes or until softened, then add the rice wine or sherry, soy sauce and sugar. Increase the heat to high and toss the ingredients vigorously to combine. Sprinkle over the white wine or cider vinegar and serve at once.

Serves 4 as an accompaniment, or as part of an oriental meal

FENNEL WITH BEAN SPROUTS AND ORANGE

2 TABLESPOONS OLIVE OIL

1 MEDIUM ONION, SLICED THINLY

2 HEADS FENNEL, SLICED THINLY, WITH ANY

LEAVES RESERVED

125 G (4 OZ) BEAN SPROUTS

PEPPER

ORANGE SLICES TO GARNISH

SAUCE:

2 TEASPOONS CORNFLOUR

4 TABLESPOONS WATER

4 TABLESPOONS ORANGE JUICE

2 TABLESPOONS SOY SAUCE

2 TABLESPOONS DRY SHERRY

First prepare the sauce ingredients: mix the cornflour to a thin paste with the water, then stir in the orange juice, soy sauce and sherry. Set aside.

Heat the wok until hot. Add the oil and heat over a moderate heat until hot. Add the onion and stir-fry for 2-3 minutes or until softened but not brown. Add the fennel, increase the heat to high and stir-fry for 3-4 minutes or until just beginning to soften.

Stir the sauce to mix, pour into the wok and bring to the boil, stirring. Add the bean sprouts and toss until all the ingredients are combined and piping hot. Add pepper to taste and serve at once, garnished with orange slices and the reserved fennel leaves, if desired.

Serves 4-6 as an accompaniment

FRESH VEGETABLE AND NUT STIR-FRY

125 G (4 OZ) CASHEW NUTS

4 MEDIUM CARROTS, SLICED THINLY INTO RINGS

ON THE DIAGONAL

4 MEDIUM COURGETTES, SLICED INTO RINGS

ON THE DIAGONAL

2 TABLESPOONS VEGETABLE OIL

1 MEDIUM ONION, SLICED THINLY

2.5 CM (1 INCH) PIECE FRESH ROOT GINGER, PEELED AND

CHOPPED FINELY

2 CLOVES GARLIC, CRUSHED

1 MEDIUM RED PEPPER, CORED, SEEDED AND CUT

LENGTHWAYS INTO THIN STRIPS

3 TABLESPOONS CASHEW NUT BUTTER

2 TABLESPOONS SOY SAUCE

½-1 TEASPOON HOT CHILLI POWDER, ACCORDING TO TASTE

1 X 227 G (7½ OZ) CAN WATER CHESTNUTS,

DRAINED AND SLICED THINLY

125 G (4 OZ) BEAN SPROUTS

SALT

Chop about one-third of the cashews and set them aside for the garnish. Blanch the carrots in boiling salted water for 2 minutes. Remove with a slotted spoon, rinse immediately under cold running water and drain. Add the courgettes to the water and blanch for 1½ minutes. Drain, reserve 300 ml (½ pint) of the blanching water, then rinse the courgettes under cold running water and drain again.

Heat the wok until hot. Add the oil and heat over a moderate heat until hot. Add the onion, ginger and garlic and stir-fry for 2-3 minutes or until softened, taking care not to let the ingredients brown. Add the red pepper and stir-fry for 2-3 minutes or until softened, then gradually stir in the reserved blanching water. Stir in the cashew nut butter, soy sauce and chilli powder. Bring to the boil, stirring constantly.

Add the carrots, courgettes, water chestnuts and bean sprouts to the wok, increase the heat to high and toss for 1-2 minutes or until all the ingredients are combined and piping hot. Add the whole cashews and toss until evenly mixed with the vegetables. Serve at once, sprinkled with the reserved chopped cashews

Serves 4 as a vegetarian main dish, with noodles or rice as an accompaniment

SPICED VEGETABLES IN COCONUT SAUCE

Take care when stir-frying with coconut milk as it does tend to stick to the bottom of the wok.

100 G (3½ OZ) CREAMED COCONUT, CHOPPED ROUGHLY

3 MEDIUM CARROTS, SLICED THINLY ON THE DIAGONAL

175 G (6 OZ) CAULIFLOWER FLORETS, BROKEN INTO SPRIGS, WITH STALKS SLICED ON THE DIAGONAL

125 G (4 OZ) GREEN BEANS, TOPPED AND TAILED AND CUT IN HALF CROSSWAYS

2 TABLESPOONS VEGETABLE OIL

1 MEDIUM ONION, CHOPPED FINELY

2.5 CM (1 INCH) PIECE FRESH ROOT GINGER, PEELED AND CHOPPED FINELY

2 CLOVES GARLIC, CRUSHED

2 TEASPOONS GROUND CORIANDER

½-1 TEASPOON HOT CHILLI POWDER, ACCORDING TO TASTE

¼ TEASPOON TURMERIC

75 G (3 OZ) FROZEN PEAS

SALT

First make the coconut milk: put the chopped coconut in a measuring jug, pour in boiling water up to the 300 ml (½ pint) mark and stir until the coconut is dissolved. Set aside.

Blanch the carrots, cauliflower and beans separately in boiling salted water, allowing 2 minutes for each type of vegetable. Drain, rinse immediately under cold running water and drain again.

Heat the wok until hot. Add the oil and heat over a moderate heat until hot. Add the onion, ginger and garlic and stir-fry for 2-3 minutes or until softened, taking care not to let the ingredients brown.

Add the coriander, chilli powder and turmeric and stir to mix. Add the carrots, cauliflower and beans, increase the heat to high and toss to mix with the flavouring ingredients.

Pour in the coconut milk and bring to the boil, stirring. Add the frozen peas and salt to taste, then stir-fry for a further 3-4 minutes or until all the vegetables are tender and coated in the sauce. If the mixture becomes too thick and starts to stick to the bottom of the wok, add a little water. Taste and add more salt if necessary. Serve at once.

Serves 4-6 as an accompaniment, 3-4 as a vegetarian main dish with accompaniments

STIR-FRIED SPINACH WITH PINE KERNELS AND RAISINS

375 G (12 OZ) FRESH YOUNG SPINACH

3 TABLESPOONS OLIVE OIL

2 CLOVES GARLIC, CRUSHED

75 G (3 OZ) RAISINS

50 G (2 OZ) PINE KERNELS

SALT AND PEPPER

Remove the stalks and any tough ribs from the spinach, then stack several leaves together, one on top of the other. Roll the stack up into a fat cigar shape, then cut crossways into shreds. Repeat with the remaining spinach.

Heat the wok until hot. Add the oil and heat over a moderate heat until hot. Add the spinach and garlic, increase the heat to high and stir-fry for 30 seconds to 1 minute, or just until the spinach begins to wilt.

Add the raisins, pine kernels and salt and pepper to taste and toss until hot and evenly combined with the spinach. Serve at once.

Serves 4 as an accompaniment

BABY CORN AND RED PEPPERS IN SWEET AND SOUR SAUCE

Some supermarkets have specialist vegetable sections where you can find such delights as miniature or 'baby' carrots, corn, cauliflowers, cabbages and mangetout. Some of these are just perfect left whole for stir-frying, especially if they are blanched briefly beforehand. This recipe is illustrated on page 2.

175 G (6 OZ) BABY CARROTS, SCRAPED IF NECESSARY

175 G (6 OZ) BABY CORN

2 TABLESPOONS VEGETABLE OIL

1 LARGE RED PEPPER, CORED, SEEDED AND CUT LENGTHWAYS INTO THIN STRIPS

1 MEDIUM ONION, SLICED THINLY

1 CLOVE GARLIC, CRUSHED

4 TABLESPOONS YELLOW BEAN SAUCE

1 TABLESPOON DRY SHERRY OR SHERRY VINEGAR

SALT AND PEPPER

FLAT LEAF PARSLEY TO GARNISH

Blanch the carrots in boiling salted water for 2 minutes. Lift out with a slotted spoon, rinse immediately under cold running water and leave to drain. Repeat with the corn.

Heat the wok until hot. Add the oil and heat over a moderate heat until hot. Add the red pepper, onion and garlic and stir-fry for 2-3 minutes or until softened, taking care not to let the ingredients brown. Add the carrots and baby corn, increase the heat to high and stir-fry for a further 3-4 minutes.

Add the yellow bean sauce and sherry or sherry vinegar and stir-fry until the sauce coats the vegetables and is piping hot. Add salt and pepper to taste and serve at once, garnished with flat leaf parsley.

Serves 4 as an accompaniment, or as part of an oriental meal

MIXED BEAN STIR-FRY

Served with a generous topping of freshly grated Parmesan cheese, and crusty French bread or Nutty Brown Rice (see recipe, page 33), this dish would make a nutritious vegetarian supper. You can ring the changes with the ingredients if you like, using different kinds of canned beans, or substituting another fresh vegetable such as mangetout or baby corn for the green beans.

175 G (6 OZ) GREEN BEANS, TOPPED AND TAILED AND CUT IN HALF CROSSWAYS

2 TABLESPOONS VEGETABLE OIL

1 MEDIUM ONION, CHOPPED FINELY

2 CLOVES GARLIC, CRUSHED

1 X 227 G (8 OZ) CAN TOMATOES

2 TABLESPOONS TOMATO PURÉE

1 TEASPOON DRIED MIXED HERBS

¼-½ TEASPOON SUGAR, ACCORDING TO TASTE

1 X 432 G (15.2 OZ) CAN CANNELLINI BEANS, DRAINED AND RINSED

1 X 432 G (15.2 OZ) CAN RED KIDNEY BEANS, DRAINED AND RINSED

2 TABLESPOONS CHOPPED FRESH BASIL

SALT AND PEPPER

Blanch the halved green beans in boiling salted water for 2 minutes. Drain, rinse immediately under cold running water and drain again.

Heat the wok until hot. Add the oil and heat over a moderate heat until hot. Add the onion and garlic and stir-fry for 2-3 minutes or until softened, taking care not to let them brown or burn.

Add the tomatoes, stir to mix with the onion and garlic and break them up with a wooden spoon. Add the tomato purée, dried herbs, sugar and salt and pepper to taste. Bring to the boil, stirring constantly.

Add the green beans and canned beans to the wok. Toss until piping hot and coated in the tomato sauce. Remove from the heat and stir in the basil. Taste for seasoning and adjust if necessary. Serve at once.

Serves 4-6 as an accompaniment, 4 as a supper dish with grated cheese, and bread or rice as an accompaniment

GARLIC MUSHROOMS

Some good supermarkets sell packets of mixed mushrooms such as brown cap, flat and oyster; these are ideal for this dish as they are more economical than buying different varieties separately, and they offer a wider choice than you would normally find in one shop. If you like, you can swirl a few tablespoons of cream, soured cream, natural yogurt or natural fromage frais over these mushrooms just before serving, then sprinkle with a little extra chopped fresh parsley.

2 TABLESPOONS OLIVE OIL

15 G (½ OZ) BUTTER

375 G (12 OZ) MIXED WILD MUSHROOMS, SLICED THINLY

3-4 CLOVES GARLIC, CRUSHED

2-3 TABLESPOONS DRY SHERRY OR VERMOUTH

4 TABLESPOONS CHOPPED FRESH PARSLEY

SALT AND PEPPER

Heat the wok until hot. Add the oil and butter and heat over a moderate heat until foaming. Add the mushrooms, garlic, salt and plenty of pepper. Increase the heat to high, sprinkle over the sherry or vermouth and stir-fry for 4-5 minutes or until the mushrooms are tender.

Taste and adjust the seasoning if necessary, then remove the wok from the heat and stir in the chopped parsley. Serve at once.

Serves 4 as an accompaniment

HOT-TOSSED CAULIFLOWER WITH ALMONDS

This recipe can be used for broccoli as well as cauliflower, with equally good results, and the almonds can be replaced with cashews or pine kernels, whichever you prefer.

1 MEDIUM CAULIFLOWER

50 G (2 OZ) BLANCHED ALMONDS

2 TABLESPOONS VEGETABLE OIL

1 MEDIUM ONION, CHOPPED FINELY

2.5 CM (1 INCH) PIECE FRESH ROOT GINGER, PEELED AND CHOPPED FINELY

2 CLOVES GARLIC, CRUSHED

2 TEASPOONS GROUND CORIANDER

1 TEASPOON TURMERIC

½ TEASPOON CHILLI POWDER

6 TABLESPOONS WATER

SALT

Break the leaves off the cauliflower and reserve the small, green frondy pieces. Separate the florets from the stalks. Break the florets into individual sprigs and slice the stalks thinly on the diagonal. Blanch the stalks and sprigs in boiling salted water for 2 minutes. Drain, rinse immediately under cold running water and drain again.

Heat the wok until hot. Add the almonds and dry-fry over a gentle heat until toasted on all sides. Remove the wok from the heat and tip the toasted almonds on to a chopping board. Chop the almonds coarsely.

Return the wok to a moderate heat. Add the oil and heat until hot. Add the onion, ginger, garlic and spices and stir-fry for 2-3 minutes or until softened, taking care not to let the ingredients brown.

Add the cauliflower sprigs and stalks and sprinkle over the water and salt to taste. Increase the heat to high and stir-fry for 2-3 minutes or until the cauliflower is tender but still crisp.

Taste and add more salt if necessary. Serve at once, sprinkled with the chopped toasted almonds and garnished with the reserved green cauliflower leaves.

Serves 4 as an accompaniment

VEGETABLE CURRY

3 MEDIUM CARROTS, SLICED THINLY ON THE DIAGONAL

175 G (6 OZ) CAULIFLOWER FLORETS, BROKEN INTO SPRIGS,

WITH STALKS SLICED ON THE DIAGONAL

125 G (4 OZ) GREEN BEANS, TOPPED AND TAILED AND CUT IN

HALF CROSSWAYS

125 G (4 OZ) PIECE MOOLI, PEELED AND SLICED THINLY

2 TABLESPOONS VEGETABLE OIL

1 SMALL ONION, CHOPPED FINELY

2.5 CM (1 INCH) PIECE FRESH ROOT GINGER, PEELED AND

CHOPPED FINELY

1 CLOVE GARLIC, CRUSHED

1 FRESH CHILLI, SEEDED AND CHOPPED FINELY

1 TEASPOON HOT CHILLI POWDER, OR TO TASTE

125 ML (4 FL OZ) WATER

3 TABLESPOONS CRUNCHY PEANUT BUTTER

125 G (4 OZ) FROZEN PEAS

SALT

40 G (1½ OZ) DRY ROASTED PEANUTS, CHOPPED, TO GARNISH

Blanch the carrots, cauliflower, beans and mooli separately in boiling salted water, allowing 2 minutes for each type of vegetable. Drain, rinse immediately under cold running water and drain again.

Heat the wok until hot. Add the oil and heat over a moderate heat until hot. Add the onion, ginger, garlic and fresh chilli and stir-fry for 2-3 minutes or until softened, taking care not to let the ingredients brown.

Add the chilli powder and stir to mix, then add the water and peanut butter. Bring to the boil, stirring, then add the blanched vegetables, the peas and salt to taste. Stir-fry for 3-4 minutes or until all the vegetables are tender.

Serve at once, sprinkled with chopped dry roasted peanuts.

Serves 4-6 as an accompaniment, 4 as a vegetarian main course with accompaniments

COURGETTES WITH CREAM AND HERBS

To cut courgettes into stick shapes, first cut the courgettes in half crossways, then slice each half lengthways into quarters.

2 TABLESPOONS OLIVE OIL

1 MEDIUM ONION, CHOPPED FINELY

2 CLOVES GARLIC, CRUSHED

15 G (½ OZ) BUTTER

500 G (1 LB) COURGETTES, TOPPED AND TAILED AND CUT

INTO THIN STRIPS

4 TABLESPOONS DRY WHITE WINE

125 ML (4 FL OZ) DOUBLE CREAM

3 TABLESPOONS CHOPPED MIXED FRESH HERBS (SUCH AS

BASIL, PARSLEY AND CHERVIL)

SALT AND PEPPER

Heat the wok until hot. Add the oil and heat over a moderate heat until hot. Add the onion and garlic and stir-fry for 2-3 minutes or until softened slightly, taking care not to let them brown or burn.

Add the butter to the wok and stir until melted, then add the courgettes and white wine, increase the heat to high and toss for 3-4 minutes or until tender.

Pour the cream into the wok and stir until it coats the courgettes. Remove the wok from the heat and stir in the chopped herbs and salt and pepper to taste. Serve at once.

Serves 4 as an accompaniment

SWEET AND SOUR LEEKS

Make sure the leeks are thoroughly clean before slicing them. The best way to do this is to slit them lengthways down their centres, then hold them open under cold running water so that the sand and grit gets washed away.

2 TABLESPOONS VEGETABLE OIL

1 ONION, CHOPPED FINELY

500 G (1 LB) LEEKS, SLICED THICKLY ON THE DIAGONAL

250 G (8 OZ) RIPE TOMATOES, SKINNED, SEEDED AND CHOPPED ROUGHLY

1 TABLESPOON TOMATO PURÉE

1 TABLESPOON CIDER VINEGAR

1 TEASPOON CASTER SUGAR

SALT AND PEPPER

Heat the wok until hot. Add the oil and heat over a moderate heat until hot. Add the onion and stir-fry for 2-3 minutes or until softened but not brown.

Add the leeks, increase the heat to high and stir-fry for 3-4 minutes or until just beginning to soften. Add the tomatoes, tomato purée, cider vinegar, sugar and salt and pepper to taste and toss for a further 3-4 minutes or until the leeks are tender. Taste and adjust the seasoning if necessary. Serve at once.
Serves 4-6 as an accompaniment, or as part of an oriental meal

MOOLI

MOOLI IS A LONG, WHITE TAPERING VEGETABLE GROWN THROUGH SOUTH EAST ASIA. IN JAPAN IT IS CALLED DAIKON, AND INDEED IT IS OFTEN REFERRED TO IN THE WEST AS 'JAPANESE WHITE RADISH'. ITS SHAPE IS UNUSUAL AND ITS COLOUR IS PURE WHITE, MAKING IT A MOST INTERESTING VEGETABLE TO LOOK AT, BUT ITS FLAVOUR IS DISAPPOINTINGLY BLAND. ORIENTAL COOKS PRIZE IT FOR ITS CRISP TEXTURE, AND USE IT FREQUENTLY IN SALADS AND AS A GARNISH CARVED AND CUT INTO BEAUTIFUL SHAPES — OR SIMPLY GRATED AND ARRANGED IN DAINTY LITTLE PILES ON THE EDGE OF A PLATE. THE JAPANESE LIKE TO EAT DAIKON BRAISED IN SHOYU (JAPANESE SOY SAUCE), MIRIN (SWEET RICE WINE) AND STOCK, SOMETIMES COMBINING IT WITH MEAT, AND EVEN WITH A LONG COOKING TIME IT STILL RETAINS ITS CRISPNESS. MOOLI CAN BE BOUGHT AT MOST LARGE SUPERMARKETS WITH GOOD FRESH VEGETABLE SECTIONS AS WELL AS IN ORIENTAL STORES.

ARTICHOKE AND RED PEPPER STIR-FRY

Roasted red pepper is soft and sweet, with a smoky 'barbecued' flavour. If you are short of time, omit the roasting of the red pepper, but you will then need to stir-fry the fresh red pepper for a few minutes longer in order to soften it.

1 LARGE RED PEPPER

2 TABLESPOONS OLIVE OIL

1 MEDIUM ONION, CHOPPED FINELY

2.5 CM (**1** INCH) PIECE FRESH ROOT GINGER, PEELED AND CHOPPED FINELY

1 CLOVE GARLIC, CRUSHED

1 X **297**G (**10½** OZ) CAN ARTICHOKE BOTTOMS, DRAINED AND SLICED

1 TABLESPOON BALSAMIC VINEGAR

SALT AND PEPPER

A FEW FRESH BASIL LEAVES TO GARNISH

Roast the red pepper under a hot grill, turning it frequently until the skin is charred black on all sides. Wrap in kitchen paper, place immediately in a polythene bag and close tightly. Leave until cold.

Unwrap the red pepper and rub off the blackened skin under cold running water. Pull out and discard the core and seeds, then cut the pepper open lengthways, rinse and pat dry with kitchen paper. Cut the pepper lengthways into thin strips then set aside.

Heat the wok until hot. Add the oil and heat over a moderate heat until hot. Add the onion, ginger and garlic and stir-fry for 2-3 minutes or until softened, taking care not to let the ingredients brown. Add the artichokes and pepper strips, increase the heat to high and toss until piping hot. Sprinkle over the balsamic vinegar and add salt and pepper to taste. Serve at once, garnished with the basil leaves.

Serves 4 as an accompaniment

CARROTS WITH CORIANDER AND ORANGE

1 TABLESPOON VEGETABLE OIL

40 G (**1½** OZ) BUTTER

1 SMALL ONION, CHOPPED FINELY

1 TEASPOON CORIANDER SEEDS, CRUSHED

500 G (**1** LB) CARROTS, SLICED THINLY ON THE DIAGONAL

FINELY GRATED RIND AND JUICE OF **1** LARGE ORANGE

1 TABLESPOON SOY SAUCE

1 TEASPOON SOFT BROWN SUGAR

2 TABLESPOONS FINELY CHOPPED FRESH CORIANDER

SALT AND PEPPER

CORIANDER SPRIGS TO GARNISH

Heat the wok until hot. Add the oil and 25 g (1 oz) of the butter and heat over a moderate heat until foaming. Add the onion and crushed coriander seeds and stir-fry for 2-3 minutes or until the onion is softened but not brown.

Add the carrots and stir well to mix, then add the orange rind and juice, the soy sauce, sugar and salt and pepper to taste. Increase the heat to high and stir-fry for 4-5 minutes or until the carrots are tender but still quite crunchy.

Add the remaining butter to the wok and stir-fry until the carrots become glazed. Remove from the heat and stir in the fresh coriander. Taste and adjust the seasoning if necessary and serve at once, garnished with coriander sprigs.

Serves 4-6 as an accompaniment

SWEET AND SOUR CUCUMBER

This simple vegetable dish is good with rich-tasting meat dishes because it is sharp and cool in flavour. It also goes well with fish.

1 MEDIUM CUCUMBER

1 TABLESPOON VEGETABLE OIL

2 TABLESPOONS WHITE WINE OR CIDER VINEGAR

2 TABLESPOONS CASTER SUGAR

SALT

Cut off the ends of the cucumber and discard, then cut the cucumber crossways into 6 equal pieces. Cut each piece of cucumber lengthways into eighths, then cut off the seeds and discard them.

Heat the wok until hot. Add the oil and heat over a moderate heat until hot. Add the wine or cider vinegar and the sugar and stir until sizzling, then add the cucumber strips and salt to taste. Stir-fry for 2-3 minutes or until the cucumber is softened but still crunchy. Serve at once.

Serves 4 as an accompaniment, or as part of an oriental meal

SWEETCORN FRITTERS

ABOUT 300 ML (½ PINT) VEGETABLE OIL

2 SPRING ONIONS, CHOPPED VERY FINELY

1 CLOVE GARLIC, CRUSHED

1 TEASPOON GROUND CORIANDER

1 TEASPOON HOT CHILLI POWDER

3 EGGS, BEATEN

1 x 340 G (12 OZ) CAN SWEETCORN KERNELS WITH PEPPERS, DRAINED THOROUGHLY

SALT

Heat the wok until hot. Add 1 tablespoon of the oil and heat over a moderate heat until hot. Add the spring onions, garlic, coriander and chilli powder and stir-fry for 30 seconds or until softened, taking care not to let the ingredients brown. Tip the contents of the wok into the beaten eggs, add the sweetcorn and peppers and salt to taste and mix well.

Wipe the inside of the wok clean with kitchen paper. Pour in the remaining oil and heat until hot but not smoking. Add level tablespoonfuls of the sweetcorn mixture to the hot oil, sliding them in carefully from the edge of the wok, and shallow-fry in batches for about 1 minute each batch until lightly browned and set on both sides. Lift out with a slotted spoon and drain on kitchen paper while shallow-frying the remaining sweetcorn mixture in the same way. Serve hot.

Makes about 20

GADO-GADO

The name 'gado-gado' sounds most intriguing to those who have not heard it before. It is in fact Indonesian for 'a mixture', or a mixed vegetable salad. Indonesians vary the ingredients according to what is freshest and best on the day, so you do not have to stick rigidly to the vegetables suggested here. In Indonesia, most cooks add a little shrimp paste (terasi) to the sauce to give it a fishy flavour. If terasi is difficult to obtain, add 1-2 teaspoons anchovy essence instead.

12 NEW POTATOES, SCRUBBED

ABOUT 600 ML (1 PINT) VEGETABLE OIL FOR DEEP-FRYING

125 G (4 OZ) SHELLED PEANUTS

6 YOUNG CARROTS, SCRUBBED AND SLICED THINLY
ON THE DIAGONAL

175 G (6 OZ) CAULIFLOWER FLORETS, BROKEN INTO SPRIGS,
WITH STALKS SLICED THINLY ON THE DIAGONAL

125 G (4 OZ) MANGETOUT, TOPS REMOVED

75 G (3 OZ) CREAMED COCONUT, CHOPPED ROUGHLY

2 CLOVES GARLIC, CHOPPED ROUGHLY

1 TEASPOON HOT CHILLI POWDER

1 TEASPOON SOFT BROWN SUGAR

JUICE OF 2 LIMES

2 LITTLE GEM LETTUCES, SEPARATED INTO LEAVES

½ CUCUMBER, SLICED VERY THINLY

3 HARD-BOILED EGGS, SLICED THINLY

125 G (4 OZ) BEAN SPROUTS

SALT

PRAWN CRACKERS (SEE RIGHT) TO GARNISH

Cook the potatoes in boiling salted water for 20 minutes or until tender.

Meanwhile, pour the oil into the wok and heat to 190°C, 375°F or until a cube of bread browns in 20-30 seconds. Add the peanuts and deep-fry for about 5 minutes or until the skins darken. Remove the peanuts from the oil with a slotted spoon and drain on kitchen paper.

Remove the potatoes from the water with a slotted spoon and leave until cool enough to handle. Meanwhile, add the carrots to the potato water, bring back to the boil and blanch for 2 minutes. Remove with a slotted spoon and set aside. Blanch the cauliflower and mangetout in the same way. Reserve the blanching water.

Put the peanuts in a food processor with the creamed coconut, garlic, chilli powder, sugar, lime juice and a few tablespoons of the vegetable blanching water. Process until a paste is formed.

Peel off the potato skins with your fingers, then slice the potatoes. Arrange the lettuce leaves decoratively around the edge of a large serving platter, then arrange all the cooked vegetables on the platter, either in groups or concentric circles, with the cucumber and hard-boiled egg slices towards the edge and the bean sprouts piled up in the centre.

Pour off all but about 1 tablespoon of the oil from the wok. Add the peanut paste and stir to mix over moderate heat. Pour in 150 ml (¼ pint) of the vegetable blanching water and bring to the boil, stirring. Pour some of the sauce over the bean sprouts and garnish with prawn crackers. Serve the salad as soon as possible, with the remaining sauce handed separately in a bowl or jug.

Serves 4-6 as a vegetarian main course

PRAWN CRACKERS

PRAWN CRACKERS ARE SOLD IN BOXES IN ORIENTAL STORES AND SOME LARGE SUPERMARKETS WITH ORIENTAL SECTIONS. THE PINKER THEY ARE THE STRONGER THEIR PRAWN FLAVOUR. THEY ARE ALWAYS SOLD IN THEIR DRIED FORM AND SHOULD BE DEEP-FRIED A HANDFUL AT A TIME IN HOT OIL UNTIL THEY PUFF UP AND BECOME CRISP AND LIGHT. (INDONESIAN PRAWN CRACKERS, CALLED 'KRUPUK', PUFF UP TO AN ENORMOUS SIZE.) DRAIN THEM WELL BEFORE SERVING - THEY ARE VERY GOOD WITH COCKTAILS OR OTHER DRINKS BEFORE AN ORIENTAL MEAL, OR THEY CAN BE USED AS AN ACCOMPANIMENT OR GARNISH TO AN ORIENTAL DISH.

SESAME MANGETOUT

2 TABLESPOONS SESAME SEEDS

2 TABLESPOONS VEGETABLE OIL

5 CM (2 INCH) PIECE FRESH ROOT GINGER, PEELED AND

CHOPPED FINELY

2 CLOVES GARLIC, CRUSHED

500 G (1 LB) MANGETOUT, TOPS REMOVED

1 X 227 G (7½ OZ) CAN WATER CHESTNUTS, DRAINED AND

SLICED THINLY

2 TABLESPOONS SOY SAUCE

1 TABLESPOON SESAME OIL

PEPPER

FLAT LEAF PARSLEY TO GARNISH

Heat the wok until hot. Add the sesame seeds and dry-fry over a gentle heat for 1-2 minutes or until toasted. Remove from the wok and set aside.

Add the vegetable oil and heat over a moderate heat until hot. Add the ginger and garlic and stir-fry for 1-2 minutes to flavour the oil, taking care not to let them brown.

Add the mangetout, increase the heat to high and stir-fry for 2 minutes. Add the water chestnuts, soy sauce and pepper to taste and toss until all the ingredients are combined and piping hot. Sprinkle over the sesame oil. Serve at once, sprinkled with the toasted sesame seeds and garnished with flat leaf parsley.

Serves 4 as an accompaniment, or as part of an oriental meal

SWEET AND SOUR VEGETABLE STIR-FRY

If you like a hot and spicy flavour, add 1-2 tablespoons bottled chilli sauce to the sauce made here, or add 1 fresh chilli, finely chopped, with the pepper strips.

2 TABLESPOONS VEGETABLE OIL

125 G (4 OZ) GREEN BEANS, TOPPED AND TAILED AND CUT

CROSSWAYS IN HALF

125 G (4 OZ) MANGETOUT, TOPS REMOVED

1 MEDIUM RED, YELLOW OR ORANGE PEPPER, CORED, SEEDED

AND CUT LENGTHWAYS INTO THIN STRIPS

125 G (4 OZ) YOUNG TENDER ASPARAGUS SPEARS, LEFT

WHOLE IF SMALL OR CUT INTO 4 CM (1½ INCH) LENGTHS ON

THE DIAGONAL

½ BUNCH SPRING ONIONS, SLICED THINLY ON THE DIAGONAL

PEPPER

SAUCE:

2 TEASPOONS CORNFLOUR

4 TABLESPOONS WATER

2 TABLESPOONS SOY SAUCE

2 TABLESPOONS RICE WINE OR DRY SHERRY

1 TABLESPOON RED OR WHITE WINE VINEGAR

1 TEASPOON CASTER SUGAR

First prepare the sauce ingredients: mix the cornflour to a thin paste with the water, then stir in the remaining sauce ingredients. Set aside.

Heat the wok until hot. Add the oil and heat over a moderate heat until hot. Add the beans and mangetout, increase the heat to high and stir-fry for 2 minutes, then add the pepper strips and stir-fry for a further 2 minutes.

Add the asparagus and spring onions and stir-fry for 2 minutes. Stir the sauce to mix, then pour into the wok and toss until all the vegetables are coated in the sauce. Add pepper to taste and serve at once.

Serves 4-6 as an accompaniment, or as part of an oriental meal

VEGETABLE CHOW MEIN

250 G (8 OZ) THREAD OR FINE EGG NOODLES

2 TABLESPOONS VEGETABLE OIL

2 CARROTS, CUT INTO MATCHSTICK STRIPS

1 GREEN PEPPER, CORED, SEEDED AND CUT LENGTHWAYS

INTO THIN STRIPS

3 CELERY STICKS, SLICED THINLY ON THE DIAGONAL

1 X 227 G (7½ OZ) CAN WATER CHESTNUTS, DRAINED AND

SLICED THINLY

175 G (6 OZ) CHINESE LEAVES, SHREDDED

175 G (6 OZ) SPINACH LEAVES, SHREDDED

PEPPER

SAUCE:

2 TEASPOONS CORNFLOUR

4 TABLESPOONS WATER

2 TABLESPOONS SOY SAUCE

1 TABLESPOON RICE WINE OR DRY SHERRY

First prepare the sauce ingredients: mix the cornflour to a thin paste with the water, then stir in the soy sauce and rice wine or sherry. Set aside.

Break the noodles into pieces with your fingers, then cook according to packet instructions.

Meanwhile, heat the wok until hot, add the oil and heat over a moderate heat until hot. Add the carrots, green pepper and celery, increase the heat to high and stir-fry for 2-3 minutes.

Stir the sauce to mix, pour into the wok and bring to the boil, stirring constantly. Remove the wok from the heat.

Drain the noodles and add to the wok. Return the wok to a high heat, add the water chestnuts, Chinese leaves and spinach and toss for 1-2 minutes or until all the ingredients are combined and the spinach is just wilted. Add pepper to taste and serve at once.

Serves 4 as a vegetarian main course

FRAGRANT RICE WITH VEGETABLES AND NUTS

'Easy-cook' rice comes in brown and white varieties, and you can use either for this recipe. Brown rice will give a nice nutty texture, but remember it takes about twice as long to cook as white rice.

250 G (8 OZ) 'EASY-COOK' LONG-GRAIN RICE

1 CINNAMON STICK

SEEDS OF 4-6 CARDAMOM PODS

3-4 CLOVES

3 TABLESPOONS VEGETABLE OIL

1 MEDIUM GREEN PEPPER, CORED, SEEDED AND

CHOPPED FINELY

1 MEDIUM ONION, CHOPPED FINELY

1 CLOVE GARLIC, CRUSHED

125 G (4 OZ) BUTTON MUSHROOMS, SLICED THINLY

125 G (4 OZ) FROZEN PEAS

175 ML (6 FL OZ) VEGETABLE STOCK MADE FROM A CUBE,

OR WATER

2 MEDIUM CARROTS, GRATED

100 G (3½ OZ) CASHEW NUTS

SALT AND PEPPER

Cook the rice in boiling salted water according to packet instructions, together with the cinnamon stick, cardamom seeds and cloves. Drain and set aside, removing the spices.

Heat the wok until hot. Add the oil and heat over a moderate heat until hot. Add the green pepper, onion and garlic and stir-fry for 2-3 minutes or until softened slightly. Add the mushrooms and frozen peas, increase the heat to high and stir-fry for 3-4 minutes or until tender.

Add the cooked rice and stock or water to the wok and toss to mix with the vegetables, then stir in the grated carrots and about three-quarters of the cashew nuts. Toss for a further minute. Add salt and pepper to taste and serve at once, sprinkled with the remaining cashew nuts.

Serves 4 as an accompaniment

TAHU GORENG

Bean curd (tofu) is the main ingredient in this famous Indonesian speciality – 'tahu' is in fact the Indonesian word for bean curd. In Indonesia, the seeds would be left in the fresh chillies to create a fiery hot dish, but you may prefer not to include all of them.

ABOUT 300 ML (½ PINT) VEGETABLE OIL FOR SHALLOW-FRYING

250 G (8 OZ) FIRM BEAN CURD (TOFU), DRAINED AND CUBED

50 G (2 OZ) NATURAL PEANUTS

4 SPRING ONIONS, CHOPPED FINELY

3 CLOVES GARLIC, CRUSHED

2 FRESH GREEN CHILLIES, CHOPPED FINELY

1 CM (½ INCH) PIECE TERASI

125 G (4 OZ) CREAMED COCONUT, GRATED OR CHOPPED FINELY

3 HEAPED TABLESPOONS CRUNCHY PEANUT BUTTER

2 TABLESPOONS SOY SAUCE

1 TEASPOOON SOFT BROWN SUGAR

300 ML (½ PINT) BOILING WATER

125 G (4 OZ) WHITE CABBAGE, SHREDDED FINELY

200 G (7 OZ) BEAN SPROUTS

TO GARNISH:

CUCUMBER STRIPS

THINLY SLICED SPRING ONIONS

Heat the oil in the wok until hot but not smoking. Add the bean curd and shallow-fry for 2-3 minutes or until golden on all sides, taking care not to let it break up. Lift out with a slotted spoon, drain and keep hot on kitchen paper. Repeat with the peanuts.

Pour off all but about 2 tablespoons oil from the wok. Add the spring onions, garlic, chillies and terasi and stir-fry over a moderate heat for 2-3 minutes or until softened, mashing the terasi to blend it with the other ingredients. Add the creamed coconut, peanut butter, soy sauce and sugar, then gradually stir in the boiling water, mixing well. Increase the heat to high and bring to the boil, stirring constantly until thickened.

Put the white cabbage and bean sprouts in a warmed serving bowl, place the fried bean curd on top and pour over the coconut sauce.

Garnish with the fried peanuts, cucumber strips and sliced spring onions and serve at once.

Serves 4 as a vegetarian main course, with rice or noodles as an accompaniment

CHINESE LEAVES

NOT TO BE CONFUSED WITH CHINESE CABBAGE OR 'BOK CHOY', WHICH HAS A MUSTARDY FLAVOUR AND LOOKS SIMILAR TO SWISS CHARD AND SPINACH, CHINESE LEAVES COME IN A TIGHTLY PACKED, LONG CYLINDER OF CRINKLY LEAVES - SIMILAR TO COS LETTUCE ONLY PALER. ALSO KNOWN AS 'PE-TSAI', CHINESE LEAVES ARE WIDELY AVAILABLE AT SUPERMARKETS AS WELL AS IN ORIENTAL STORES, AND ARE EXCELLENT IN STIR-FRIES BECAUSE THEY RETAIN THEIR CRISPNESS AND COLOUR. UNLIKE MOST GREEN VEGETABLES, THEY KEEP WELL, SO ARE HANDY TO HAVE IN THE REFRIGERATOR AS THEY CAN BE EATEN RAW IN SALADS AS WELL AS BEING COOKED IN STIR-FRIES.

RICE & NOODLES

No oriental meal seems complete without a bowl of rice or noodles, and everyone loves them, so it's good to have a repertoire of recipes to choose from. From traditional to modern, there are rice and noodle dishes to suit all tastes.

VELVET NOODLES WITH CRAB

250 G (8 OZ) FRESH OR DRIED TAGLIATELLE NOODLES

1 TABLESPOON SESAME OIL

175 G (6 OZ) BROCCOLI, BROKEN INTO SPRIGS, STALKS SLICED

3 TABLESPOONS VEGETABLE OIL

5 CM (2 INCH) PIECE FRESH ROOT GINGER, PEELED AND CRUSHED

2 CLOVES GARLIC, CRUSHED

375 G (12 OZ) WHITE CRAB MEAT, FLAKED

SALT AND PEPPER

SOY SAUCE TO SERVE

SAUCE:

150 ML (¼ PINT) FISH STOCK (SEE PAGE 29)

4 TABLESPOONS SOY SAUCE

2 TABLESPOONS DRY SHERRY OR WHITE WINE

Cook the tagliatelle in boiling salted water, according to packet instructions. Drain thoroughly, place in a bowl and toss with the sesame oil. Cover and keep hot.

Blanch the broccoli in boiling salted water for 1½ minutes. Drain, rinse immediately under cold water and drain again.

Prepare the sauce ingredients: mix the fish stock in a jug or bowl with the soy sauce and sherry or white wine. Set aside.

Heat the wok until hot. Add the vegetable oil and heat over a moderate heat until hot. Add the ginger and garlic and stir-fry for 30 seconds to flavour the oil; don't let them brown. Add the broccoli, increase the heat to high and stir-fry for 3-4 minutes. Add the sauce and noodles and toss until evenly mixed. Add the crab and toss until piping hot. Add pepper to taste and serve at once. Hand soy sauce separately.

Serves 3-4 as a main dish, 4-6 as part of an oriental meal

THAI NOODLES WITH PRAWNS

Nam pla is bottled fish sauce, made from salted fish. It is available in oriental stores, but if you cannot get it you can use anchovy essence and a drop or two of vinegar instead. Raw 'tiger' prawn tails can be bought at good fishmongers and large supermarkets with specialist fresh fish counters.

250 G (8 OZ) VERMICELLI NOODLES

2 TABLESPOONS VEGETABLE OIL

125 G (4 OZ) RADISHES, TRIMMED AND SLICED THINLY

375 G (12 OZ) RAW 'TIGER' PRAWN TAILS, DEFROSTED AND DRIED THOROUGHLY, IF FROZEN, PEELED

JUICE OF 1 LEMON

1 TABLESPOON CASTER SUGAR

2 TEASPOONS NAM PLA

1 TEASPOON HOT CHILLI POWDER, OR ACCORDING TO TASTE

SALT

Cook the vermicelli in boiling salted water according to packet instructions.

Meanwhile, heat the wok until hot. Add the oil and heat over a moderate heat until hot. Add the radishes, increase the heat to high and stir-fry for 30 seconds. Add the prawns and stir-fry for 1-2 minutes or until they turn pink. Add the lemon juice, sugar, nam pla and chilli powder and stir-fry for 1-2 minutes until all the ingredients are combined and piping hot.

Drain the vermicelli and add to the prawn mixture. Toss until evenly mixed. Serve at once.

Serves 2-3 as a main dish, 4 as part of an oriental meal

CHINESE FRIED RICE

For successful fried rice, it is essential that the rice is cold before you start.

250 G (8 OZ) LONG-GRAIN RICE

750 ML (1¼ PINTS) WATER

2 EGGS

4 SPRING ONIONS, CHOPPED FINELY

2½ TABLESPOONS VEGETABLE OIL

125 G (4 OZ) FROZEN PEAS

125 G (4 OZ) BEAN SPROUTS

125 G (4 OZ) COOKED HAM, SHREDDED

2 TABLESPOONS SOY SAUCE

SALT AND PEPPER

Rinse the rice in a sieve under cold running water, then place in a medium saucepan. Add the measured water and salt to taste and bring to the boil. Stir once, cover with a lid and simmer for 15-20 minutes, or until the water is absorbed by the rice. Remove the pan from the heat, turn the rice into a sieve and rinse under cold running water. Set aside.

Beat the eggs with half of the spring onions and salt and pepper to taste. Heat the wok until hot. Add 2 teaspoons of the oil, and heat over a moderate heat until hot. Add the egg and spring onion mixture and stir until the eggs are scrambled, then remove the wok from the heat, turn the scrambled eggs into a bowl and set aside.

Return the wok to the heat, add the remaining oil and heat until hot. Add the remaining spring onions and the frozen peas, increase the heat to high and stir-fry for 2-3 minutes or until the peas are cooked.

Add the bean sprouts and stir-fry for 1 minute, then add the cold rice, scrambled eggs, ham and soy sauce. Toss for about 2 minutes or until all the ingredients are combined and piping hot, using chopsticks to help separate the grains of rice. Taste and adjust the seasoning if necessary. Serve at once.

Serves 3 as a main dish, 4 as part of an oriental meal

ANTS CLIMBING TREES

This strange-sounding Chinese dish gets its name from the minced pork (ants) clinging to the trees (noodles). In this recipe, transparent or cellophane noodles are used. Made from mung beans and called 'mien', they are sold in skeins like wool. They can be bought in oriental stores, but if you have difficulty in getting them, you can use egg noodles instead – cook them according to packet instructions. This dish is quite spicy, but if you like really hot Chinese food, add more chilli sauce, or add 1-2 finely chopped fresh chillies to the pork mixture when stir-frying.

250 G (8 OZ) TRANSPARENT OR CELLOPHANE NOODLES

250 G (8 OZ) MINCED PORK

2 TABLESPOONS VEGETABLE OIL

4 SPRING ONIONS, SLICED THINLY ON THE DIAGONAL

175 ML (6 FL OZ) HOT CHICKEN STOCK

MARINADE:

2 TABLESPOONS SOY SAUCE

1 TABLESPOON RICE WINE OR DRY SHERRY

1 TABLESPOON VEGETABLE OIL

2 TEASPOONS HOT CHILLI SAUCE

1 TEASPOON SESAME OIL

½ TEASPOON SUGAR

Soak the noodles in hot water for 30 minutes, or according to packet instructions.

Meanwhile, make the marinade: put all the ingredients in a shallow dish, add the minced pork and stir well to mix. Cover and leave to marinate for about 30 minutes.

Drain the noodles. Heat the wok until hot. Add the oil and heat over a moderate heat until hot. Add the spring onions and stir-fry for 30 seconds or until softened, taking care not to let them brown. Add the pork and marinade, increase the heat to high and stir-fry for 2-3 minutes or until the pork loses its pink colour.

Pour in the stock and bring to the boil, stirring constantly. Add the drained noodles and toss until all of the liquid is absorbed and the noodles are piping hot. Serve at once.

Serves 3-4 as a main dish, 4-6 as part of an oriental meal

CHOW MEIN

This dish, which literally translated means 'stir-fried noodles', is well known to everyone who eats in Chinese restaurants. Originally invented by Chinese immigrants in America, the noodles are now cooked all over the Western world, and with almost any meat, fish or vegetable added to them – there are no hard-and-fast rules for making chow mein.

250 G (8 OZ) CHINESE RICE NOODLES (MIHUN)

2 TABLESPOONS VEGETABLE OIL

3-4 SPRING ONIONS, SLICED THINLY ON THE DIAGONAL

2.5 CM (1 INCH) PIECE FRESH ROOT GINGER, PEELED AND
CHOPPED FINELY

1 CLOVE GARLIC, CRUSHED

2 SKINNED AND BONED CHICKEN BREASTS, EACH WEIGHING
ABOUT 150 G (5 OZ), CUT INTO THIN STRIPS ACROSS
THE GRAIN

125 G (4 OZ) MANGETOUT, TOPS REMOVED

125 G (4 OZ) LEAN SLICED COOKED HAM, SHREDDED

75 G (3 OZ) BEAN SPROUTS

PEPPER

SAUCE:

2 TEASPOONS CORNFLOUR

8 TABLESPOONS COLD CHICKEN STOCK OR WATER

2 TABLESPOONS SOY SAUCE

2 TABLESPOONS RICE WINE OR DRY SHERRY

2 TEASPOONS SESAME OIL

Cook the rice noodles according to packet instructions.

Meanwhile, prepare the sauce ingredients: mix the cornflour to a paste with 2 tablespoons of the stock or water, then stir in the remaining stock or water, the soy sauce, rice wine or sherry and the sesame oil. Set aside.

Drain the noodles, rinse under cold water and set aside.

Heat the wok until hot. Add the oil and heat over a moderate heat until hot. Add the spring onions, ginger and garlic and stir-fry for 1-2 minutes or until softened, taking care not to let the ingredients brown. Add the chicken, increase the heat to high and stir-fry for 3-4 minutes or until lightly coloured on all sides.

Add the mangetout and stir-fry for 1-2 minutes or until just tender, then add the ham and bean sprouts and stir-fry to mix. Stir the sauce to mix, pour into the wok and bring to the boil, stirring constantly. Add the drained noodles and toss until combined and piping hot. Add pepper to taste; serve at once.

Serves 4 as a main dish

SPAGHETTI WITH SPICY MINCED PORK

Minced pork is available at most supermarkets, but if you cannot find it you can use minced beef or lamb instead.

2 TABLESPOONS VEGETABLE OIL

1 SMALL ONION, CHOPPED FINELY

375 G (12 OZ) MINCED PORK

1 x 396 G (14 OZ) CAN CHOPPED TOMATOES

100 ML (3½ FL OZ) CHICKEN STOCK MADE FROM A CUBE,
OR WATER

2 TABLESPOONS SOY SAUCE

2 TABLESPOONS TOMATO PURÉE

1 TEASPOON CHILLI POWDER, OR TO TASTE

½ TEASPOON FIVE-SPICE POWDER

¼ TEASPOON SUGAR

250 G (8 OZ) SPAGHETTI

SALT

Heat the wok until hot. Add the oil and heat over a moderate heat until hot. Add the onion and stir-fry for 2-3 minutes or until softened slightly, taking care not to let the onion brown.

Add the pork, increase the heat to high and stir-fry for 3-4 minutes or until it changes colour.

Add the chopped tomatoes, chicken stock, soy sauce, tomato purée, chilli and five-spice powders and sugar and bring to the boil, stirring. Lower the heat, cover the wok with a lid and cook for 10-15 minutes or until the pork mixture is reduced and thickened, stirring frequently.

Meanwhile, cook the spaghetti in a separate pan of boiling salted water for 12 minutes, or according to packet instructions.

Drain the spaghetti well, then tip into the wok. Increase the heat to high and toss to combine with the meat and tomato sauce. Serve at once.

Serves 4 as a main dish

SINGAPORE NOODLES WITH HOT SAUCE

This recipe is simple and quick to make, relying as it does on bottled chilli sauce for its main flavouring. Take care when using chilli sauce for the first time, because some brands are fiery hot while others are milder and sometimes quite sweet. Do not be surprised to find tomato ketchup in this recipe – it is a common ingredient in Western-influenced Singapore.

250 G (8 OZ) MEDIUM EGG NOODLES

1 TABLESPOON SESAME OIL

2 TABLESPOONS VEGETABLE OIL

½ BUNCH SPRING ONIONS, SLICED THINLY ON THE DIAGONAL

1-2 GARLIC CLOVES, ACCORDING TO TASTE, CRUSHED

375 G (12 OZ) PORK FILLET (TENDERLOIN), CUT INTO THIN STRIPS ACROSS THE GRAIN

SALT

SPRING ONION TASSELS (SEE PAGE 73) TO GARNISH (OPTIONAL)

SAUCE:

90 ML (3 FL OZ) TOMATO KETCHUP

ABOUT 2 TABLESPOONS HOT CHILLI SAUCE, TO TASTE

150 ML (¼ PINT) HOT WATER

Cook the noodles according to packet instructions. Drain well, place in a bowl and sprinkle over the sesame oil. Toss to coat, cover and set aside.

Prepare the sauce ingredients: put the ketchup in a jug or bowl, add chilli sauce to taste, then stir in the water until evenly mixed. Set aside.

Heat the wok until hot. Add the vegetable oil and heat over a moderate heat until hot. Add the spring onions and garlic and stir-fry for 1-2 minutes or until softened, taking care not to let them brown.

Add the pork, increase the heat to high and stir-fry for 3-4 minutes or until browned on all sides. Add the sauce and stir until evenly mixed with the pork, then add the noodles and toss until piping hot. Taste and add more chilli sauce, and salt, if necessary. Serve at once, garnished with spring onion tassels if liked.

Serves 3 as a main dish

MEE KROB

150 G (5 OZ) GREEN BEANS, CUT CROSSWAYS IN HALF

ABOUT 600 ML (1 PINT) VEGETABLE OIL FOR DEEP-FRYING, PLUS EXTRA 2 TABLESPOONS

1 MEDIUM ONION, CHOPPED FINELY

2 CLOVES GARLIC, CRUSHED

2 SKINNED AND BONED CHICKEN BREASTS, ABOUT 150 G (5 OZ) EACH, CUT INTO STRIPS ACROSS THE GRAIN

1 TEASPOON HOT CHILLI POWDER, OR TO TASTE

250 G (8 OZ) PEELED COOKED PRAWNS, DEFROSTED AND DRIED THOROUGHLY, IF FROZEN

3 TABLESPOONS SOY SAUCE

2 TABLESPOONS NAM PLA (FISH SAUCE)

1 TABLESPOON VINEGAR

2 TEASPOONS SUGAR

250 G (8 OZ) RICE VERMICELLI

SALT

TO GARNISH:

ABOUT 50 G (2 OZ) BEAN SPROUTS

SHREDDED RIND OF 2 LIMES OR 1 ORANGE

RED CHILLI FLOWERS (SEE PAGE 109)

FRESH CORIANDER LEAVES

Blanch the beans in boiling salted water for 2 minutes. Drain, rinse under cold running water and drain again. Set aside.

Heat the wok until hot. Add the 2 tablespoons oil and heat until hot. Add the onion and garlic and stir-fry for 1-2 minutes until softened, taking care not to let them brown.

Add the chicken strips, increase the heat and stir-fry for 3-4 minutes or until lightly coloured. Sprinkle over the chilli powder, then add the prawns and stir-fry 1 minute. Add the soy and fish sauces, the vinegar and sugar and mix well. Tip the contents of the wok into a bowl, cover and keep warm.

Wipe the wok clean with kitchen paper, pour in the oil for Deep-frying and heat to 180°C-190°C, 350°F-375°F or until a cube of bread browns in 30 seconds. Deep-fry the vermicelli a handful at a time, just until they swell and puff up (do not let them colour). Remove with a slotted spoon and drain on kitchen paper. Keep hot while deep-frying the remainder.

Quickly pour off all the oil from the wok and wipe clean again. Return the wok to a high heat, add the chicken and prawn mixture and the beans and toss quickly to warm through. Add three-quarters of the vermicelli and toss for a further 30 seconds or so. Transfer to a serving platter. Garnish with the remaining vermicelli and other suggested garnishes and serve.

Serves 4 as a main dish

COCONUT RICE

Coconut rice – rice that is cooked in coconut milk rather than water – is quite tricky to make because coconut milk is very rich and tends to make the rice stick to the bottom of the wok. Sticky rice is more popular in the East than in the West (for one thing it is easier to eat with chopsticks), so don't worry if your grains of rice are not beautifully separate – they are not meant to be.

1 x 200 G (7 OZ) PACKET CREAMED COCONUT, CHOPPED ROUGHLY

250 G (8 OZ) LONG-GRAIN RICE

1 STEM LEMON GRASS, BRUISED, OR THINLY PARED RIND OF 1 LARGE LEMON

2 CURRY LEAVES OR BAY LEAVES

LARGE PINCH OF SAFFRON THREADS

SALT

FRIED ONION RINGS TO GARNISH (SEE PAGE 69) (OPTIONAL)

First make the coconut milk: put the chopped coconut in a measuring jug, pour in boiling water up to the 750 ml (1¼ pint) mark and stir until the coconut is dissolved.

Rinse the rice in a sieve under cold running water, then place in the wok. Add the coconut milk, lemon grass or lemon rind, curry or bay leaves, saffron and salt to taste. Bring to the boil over a moderate heat, stirring constantly.

Turn the heat down to its lowest setting, cover the wok with a lid and cook over a very gentle heat for 15 minutes, stirring frequently. If the mixture becomes too thick and starts to stick to the bottom of the wok, add a little water.

Remove the wok from the heat and leave to stand, still covered with its lid, for 10-15 minutes. When ready to serve, turn the rice into a warmed deep serving dish, fluff up the grains with a fork, and garnish with fried onion rings, if liked.

Serves 4 as an accompaniment, or as part of an oriental meal

HOT-TOSSED RICE SALAD

'Easy-cook' rice is best for this warm salad because the grains need to be separate or they will not become coated in the dressing.

250 G (8 OZ) 'EASY-COOK' LONG-GRAIN RICE

2 TABLESPOONS VEGETABLE OIL

1 SMALL ONION, CHOPPED FINELY

2.5 CM (1 INCH) PIECE FRESH ROOT GINGER, PEELED AND CHOPPED FINELY (OPTIONAL)

1 MEDIUM GREEN OR RED PEPPER, CORED, SEEDED AND DICED

250 G (8 OZ) PEELED COOKED PRAWNS, DEFROSTED AND DRIED THOROUGHLY, IF FROZEN

2-3 MEDIUM CARROTS, COARSELY GRATED

SALT AND PEPPER

DRESSING:

3 TABLESPOONS OLIVE OIL

1 TABLESPOON LEMON JUICE

1 CLOVE GARLIC, CRUSHED

Cook the rice in boiling salted water according to packet instructions.

Meanwhile, make the dressing: put the olive oil, lemon juice and garlic in a jug or bowl and whisk with a fork until thickened. Add salt and pepper to taste and set aside.

Heat the wok until hot. Add the oil and heat over a moderate heat until hot. Add the onion and ginger (if using) and stir-fry for 2-3 minutes or until softened, taking care not to let them brown.

Add the diced pepper and stir-fry for 2-3 minutes or until just beginning to soften, then add the prawns, increase the heat to high and stir-fry for about 2 minutes or until hot.

Tip the rice into the wok and stir to mix with the vegetables and prawns. Add the grated carrots, pour over the dressing and toss well. Taste and adjust the seasoning if necessary. Serve hot.

Serves 3-4 as a main dish

TEN-VARIETY FRIED RICE

This Thai dish is given its name 'Ten-Variety' from the number of ingredients that are added to the rice.

175 G (6 OZ) LONG-GRAIN WHITE RICE

600 ML (1 PINT) WATER

2 EGGS

3½ TABLESPOONS VEGETABLE OIL

1 SKINNED AND BONED LARGE CHICKEN BREAST, WEIGHING ABOUT 175 G (6 OZ), CUT INTO THIN STRIPS ACROSS THE GRAIN

125-175 G (4-6 OZ) PORK FILLET (TENDERLOIN), CUT INTO THIN STRIPS ACROSS THE GRAIN

1 LARGE RED PEPPER, CORED, SEEDED AND CHOPPED FINELY

4 SPRING ONIONS, SLICED THINLY ON THE DIAGONAL

2 CLOVES GARLIC, CRUSHED

3 FRESH GREEN CHILLIES, SEEDED AND CHOPPED FINELY

3 TOMATOES, CHOPPED ROUGHLY

125 G (4 OZ) PEELED COOKED PRAWNS, DEFROSTED AND DRIED THOROUGHLY, IF FROZEN

125 G (4 OZ) WHITE CRAB MEAT, FLAKED

SALT AND PEPPER

SAUCE:

150 ML (¼ PINT) FISH STOCK (SEE PAGE 29) OR FISH STOCK MADE FROM A CUBE

2 TABLESPOONS SOY SAUCE

1 TABLESPOON CASTER SUGAR

2 TEASPOONS LEMON JUICE

2 TEASPOONS NAM PLA (FISH SAUCE) OR 1 TEASPOON ANCHOVY ESSENCE

TO GARNISH:

SPRING ONIONS

CUCUMBER SLICES

CHILLI FLOWERS (SEE RIGHT)

Rinse the rice in a sieve under cold running water, then place in a medium saucepan. Add the measured water and salt to taste and bring to the boil. Stir once, cover with a lid and simmer for 15-20 minutes, or until the water is absorbed by the rice. Remove the pan from the heat, turn the rice into a sieve and rinse under cold running water. Set aside.

Beat the eggs with salt and pepper to taste. Heat 1½ teaspoons oil in an omelette pan, add the eggs and make an omelette in the usual way. Slide the omelette on to a board and roll up tightly. Set aside.

Mix all the sauce ingredients together in a bowl. Set aside.

Heat the wok until hot. Add 2 tablespoons of the remaining oil and heat over a moderate heat until hot. Add the chicken and pork, increase the heat to high and stir-fry for 3-4 minutes or until lightly coloured on all sides. Remove the wok from the heat and tip the contents into a bowl. Set aside.

Return the wok to a moderate heat, add the remaining oil and heat until hot. Add the red pepper, spring onions, garlic and chillies and stir-fry for 2-3 minutes or until softened, taking care not to let the ingredients brown. Add the tomatoes and cooked rice and stir well to mix, then return the chicken and pork and their juices to the wok and increase the heat to high. Pour in the sauce and toss until all the ingredients are combined and piping hot, using chopsticks to help separate the grains of rice.

Fold in the prawns and crab meat gently, taking care not to break up the crab, then heat through, shaking the wok occasionally. Taste for seasoning and serve at once, garnished with spring onions, cucumber slices and chilli flowers.

Serves 3-4 as a main dish, 4-6 as part of an oriental meal

CHILLI FLOWERS

CHILLI FLOWERS MAKE AN ATTRACTIVE GARNISH FOR ORIENTAL FOOD. THEY ARE SIMPLE AND QUICK TO MAKE, BUT REMEMBER ALWAYS TO WEAR RUBBER GLOVES WHEN HANDLING CHILLIES AS THEY CONTAIN AN ALKALOID CALLED 'CAPSAICIN', WHICH CAN IRRITATE THE SKIN IF IT GETS ON YOUR HANDS — OR WORSE STILL, IN YOUR EYES.

WITH A SHARP, POINTED KNIFE, CUT THE CHILLI (RED OR GREEN) LENGTHWAYS INTO 4 SECTIONS, CUTTING FROM THE BASE OF THE CHILLI TO THE TIP. DO NOT CUT RIGHT THROUGH THE BASE BECAUSE THE CHILLI MUST REMAIN INTACT. WITH THE POINT OF THE KNIFE, CAREFULLY SCRAPE OUT THE CHILLI SEEDS, THEN DROP THE CHILLIES INTO A BOWL OF ICED WATER AND PLACE IN THE REFRIGERATOR. LEAVE TO CHILL FOR AT LEAST 30 MINUTES, UNTIL THE SECTIONS OPEN AND CURL OUT LIKE THE PETALS OF A FLOWER. DRAIN WELL BEFORE USE.

RAINBOW RICE

175 G (6 OZ) LONG-GRAIN RICE

600 ML (1 PINT) WATER

2 TABLESPOONS VEGETABLE OIL

2 MEDIUM CARROTS, DICED

½ BUNCH SPRING ONIONS, CHOPPED FINELY

1 MEDIUM RED PEPPER, CORED, SEEDED AND DICED

2 CELERY STICKS, DICED

125 G (4 OZ) FROZEN PEAS

1 x 125-175 G (4-6 OZ) SLICE BOILED HAM, CUT INTO
THIN STRIPS

1 x 200 G (7 OZ) CAN WHOLE BABY MUSHROOMS IN
BRINE, DRAINED

2 TABLESPOONS SOY SAUCE

1 TABLESPOON SESAME OIL

SALT AND PEPPER

Rinse the rice in a sieve under cold running water, then place in a medium saucepan. Add the water and ½ teaspoon salt and bring to the boil. Stir once, cover with a lid and simmer for 20 minutes, or until the water is absorbed by the rice. Remove the pan from the heat, turn the rice into a sieve and rinse under cold running water. Set aside.

Heat the wok until hot. Add the vegetable oil and heat over a moderate heat until hot. Add the carrots and stir-fry for 2 minutes, then add the spring onions, red pepper and celery and stir-fry for a further 2 minutes. Add the frozen peas and ham, increase the heat to high and stir-fry for 2-3 minutes, then add the mushrooms and toss until piping hot.

Add the rice to the wok and stir-fry until evenly mixed with the ham and vegetables, using chopsticks to help separate the grains of rice. Add pepper to taste, sprinkle over the soy sauce and sesame oil and serve at once.

Serves 3-4 as a main dish, or 4-6 as part of an oriental meal

NASI GORENG

250 G (8 OZ) LONG-GRAIN RICE

750 ML (1¼ PINTS) WATER

2 EGGS

2½ TABLESPOONS VEGETABLE OIL

1 SMALL ONION, CHOPPED ROUGHLY

2 CLOVES GARLIC, CHOPPED ROUGHLY

1 FRESH GREEN CHILLI, CHOPPED ROUGHLY

1 CM (½ INCH) PIECE TERASI, OR 1-2 TEASPOONS ANCHOVY
ESSENCE, ACCORDING TO TASTE

250 G (8 OZ) BONELESS LEAN COOKED CHICKEN, PORK OR
BEEF, CUT INTO THIN STRIPS

250 G (8 OZ) PEELED COOKED PRAWNS, DEFROSTED AND
DRIED THOROUGHLY, IF FROZEN

ABOUT 3 TABLESPOONS SOY SAUCE, ACCORDING TO TASTE

SALT AND PEPPER

TO GARNISH:

PRAWN CRACKERS

FRIED ONION RINGS (SEE PAGE 69)

FRESH CHILLI RINGS

FRESH CORIANDER LEAVES

Rinse the rice under cold running water, then place in a pan. Add the measured water and salt and bring to the boil. Stir once, cover and simmer for 15-20 minutes, or until the water is absorbed. Remove from the heat, turn the rice into a sieve and rinse under cold running water. Set aside.

Beat the eggs and season to taste. Heat 1½ teaspoons oil in an omelette pan, add the eggs and make an omelette in the usual way. Slide the omelette on to a board and roll up tightly. Set aside. Pound the onion, garlic, chilli and terasi (if using) in a mortar and pestle.

Heat the wok until hot. Add the remaining oil and heat over a moderate heat until hot. Add the pounded mixture (with the anchovy essence if using) and stir-fry for 2-3 minutes, taking care not to let the ingredients brown.

Add the meat, increase the heat and stir-fry for 1-2 minutes or until hot. Add the prawns and stir-fry for a further minute.

Tip the cooked rice into the wok and stir-fry for 1-2 minutes or until the rice is mixed with the meat and prawns, using chopsticks to help separate the grains. Sprinkle over soy sauce to taste. Transfer the nasi goreng to a serving platter. Quickly cut the rolled omelette into thin rings and arrange on top of the nasi goreng. Garnish with prawn crackers, onion and chilli rings and coriander leaves. Serve at once.

Serves 3-4 as a main dish, or 4 as part of an oriental meal

MEE GORENG

This is a Singaporean noodle dish, which in its native land is made with fresh yellow wheat noodles called 'hokkien mee'. Dried egg noodles make an acceptable substitute here. In Singapore, noodle dishes are often garnished with strips of omelette. If you would like to do this, use the quantities and instructions for making these in the recipe for Nasi Goreng (see page 110).

250 G (8 OZ) MEDIUM EGG NOODLES

ABOUT 300 ML (½ PINT) VEGETABLE OIL FOR

SHALLOW-FRYING

250 G (8 OZ) FIRM BEAN CURD (TOFU), DRAINED AND CUT

INTO CUBES

½ BUNCH SPRING ONIONS, SLICED THINLY ON THE DIAGONAL

1-2 FRESH CHILLIES, SEEDED AND CHOPPED FINELY,

ACCORDING TO TASTE

1 CLOVE GARLIC, CRUSHED

2 TABLESPOONS YELLOW BEAN SAUCE

SALT

Cook the noodles according to packet instructions. Drain well, place in a bowl and sprinkle over about 1 tablespoon of the oil. Toss to coat, cover and set aside.

Heat the remaining oil in the wok until hot but not smoking. Add the bean curd and shallow-fry for 2-3 minutes or until golden on all sides, taking care not to let it break up. Lift out the bean curd with a slotted spoon, drain and keep hot on kitchen paper.

Pour off all but about 2 tablespoons of the oil from the wok. Add the spring onions, chillies and garlic and stir-fry for 30 seconds or until just softened, taking care not to let them brown. Add the yellow bean sauce and stir to mix, then add the noodles and increase the heat to high. Toss until all the ingredients are combined and piping hot, adding the bean curd for the last moment or two. Taste and add salt if necessary, then serve.

Serves 2-3 as a light supper or lunch dish, 3-4 as an accompaniment

THAI FRIED RICE

The prawns are not essential, but the combination of meat and fish is very tasty, and extremely popular in the Far East. Nam pla (fish sauce) is an essential ingredient in Thai cooking. You can buy it in bottles in oriental stores specializing in South-East Asian food, and it is well worth buying because it keeps indefinitely and can be added to all sorts of savoury foods to give them an oriental flavour.

250 G (8 OZ) LONG-GRAIN RICE

750 ML (1¼ PINTS) WATER

1 SMALL ONION, CHOPPED ROUGHLY

1 CLOVE GARLIC, CHOPPED ROUGHLY

3 DRIED RED CHILLIES, CHOPPED ROUGHLY

A FEW SPRIGS OF CORIANDER

JUICE OF 1 LIME

ABOUT 2 TABLESPOONS NAM PLA (FISH SAUCE),

ACCORDING TO TASTE

2 TABLESPOONS VEGETABLE OIL

250 G (8 OZ) BONELESS COOKED CHICKEN, PORK OR BEEF,

CUT INTO THIN STRIPS

125 G (4 OZ) PEELED COOKED PRAWNS, DEFROSTED AND

DRIED THOROUGHLY, IF FROZEN

1 TEASPOON CASTER SUGAR, OR TO TASTE

SALT

FRESH CORIANDER TO GARNISH

Rinse the rice in a sieve under cold running water, then place in a medium saucepan. Add the measured water and salt to taste and bring to the boil. Stir once, cover with a lid and simmer for 15-20 minutes, or until the water is absorbed by the rice. Remove the pan from the heat, turn the rice into a sieve and rinse under cold running water. Set aside.

Put the onion, garlic, chillies, coriander, lime juice and nam pla in a food processor and work to a paste.

Heat the wok until hot. Add the oil and heat over a moderate heat until hot. Add the spice paste and stir-fry for 2-3 minutes, then add the cooked rice, increase the heat to high and toss well, using chopsticks to help separate the grains.

Add the meat and prawns, sprinkle over sugar to taste and stir-fry for 1-2 minutes longer or until all the ingredients are combined and piping hot. Taste and add more nam pla and/or salt if necessary, with more sugar if you like. Serve hot, garnished with fresh coriander.

Serves 4 as a main dish

CURRIED RICE

It is important to rinse basmati rice well before cooking, to wash away excess starch. Some cooks even soak the rice first for about 1 hour before rinsing, which you can do as well if you have the time.

300 G (10 OZ) BASMATI RICE

2 TABLESPOONS VEGETABLE OIL

1 TABLESPOON GHEE OR BUTTER

1 MEDIUM ONION, CHOPPED FINELY

2.5 CM (1 INCH) PIECE FRESH ROOT GINGER, PEELED

AND CRUSHED

1 CLOVE GARLIC, CRUSHED

2 TEASPOONS TURMERIC

2 TEASPOONS GARAM MASALA

ABOUT 900 ML (1½ PINTS) BOILING WATER

3 CLOVES

3 CARDAMOM PODS, SPLIT

SALT

TO GARNISH:

FLAKED ALMONDS

SULTANAS

Pick over the rice and remove any pieces of grit. Put the rice in a sieve and rinse under cold running water until the water runs clear. Drain well.

Heat the wok until hot. Add the oil and ghee or butter and heat over a moderate heat until foaming. Add the onion, ginger and garlic and stir-fry for 2-3 minutes or until softened, taking care not to let them brown. Add the turmeric and garam masala and stir-fry for 1 minute, then add the rice and stir until coated in the spice mixture.

Slowly stir in the boiling water (take care and stand back as the mixture will splash and sputter). Add the cloves, cardamoms and salt to taste and bring to the boil, stirring.

Lower the heat and simmer the rice for 10 minutes, stirring frequently. Cover the wok with a lid, remove from the heat and leave to stand for 20 minutes, without removing the lid. Taste and add more salt if necessary. Serve hot, sprinkled with almonds and sultanas.

Serves 4-6 as an accompaniment

RAPID-FRIED PRAWNS WITH NOODLES

Bottled sweet and sour sauce is available at most large supermarkets as well as in oriental stores. If you like, you can add a splash or two of dry sherry, to give the sauce an extra kick. The addition of noodles makes this dish a complete meal in itself.

250 G (8 OZ) MEDIUM EGG NOODLES

2 TABLESPOONS VEGETABLE OIL

1 MEDIUM ONION, CHOPPED FINELY

1 LARGE GREEN PEPPER, CORED, SEEDED AND DICED

250 G (8 OZ) FROZEN PEELED COOKED PRAWNS

½ X 160 G (5½ OZ) BOTTLE 'STIR-FRY'

SWEET AND SOUR SAUCE

PEPPER

Put the noodles in a saucepan, pour over boiling water to cover, then cover the pan tightly with its lid. Leave to soak for 6 minutes, or according to packet instructions.

Meanwhile, heat the wok until hot. Add the oil and heat over a moderate heat until hot. Add the onion and green pepper and stir-fry for for 3-4 minutes or until softened. Add the prawns, increase the heat to high and stir-fry for 2-3 minutes or until defrosted. Pour in the sweet and sour sauce, stir to mix with the prawns and vegetables, then bring to the boil. Remove the wok from the heat.

Drain the noodles and add to the wok, stirring to mix with the prawns and vegetables. Return the wok to a high heat and toss the ingredients until evenly combined. Add pepper to taste and serve at once.

Serves 3-4 as a main dish

INDONESIAN FESTIVAL RICE

100 G (3½ OZ) CREAMED COCONUT, CHOPPED ROUGHLY

375 G (12 OZ) LONG-GRAIN RICE

2 TABLESPOONS VEGETABLE OIL

2 MEDIUM ONIONS, CHOPPED FINELY

2 CLOVES GARLIC, CRUSHED

1 TEASPOON TURMERIC

1 STEM LEMON GRASS, BRUISED, OR THINLY PARED RIND

OF 1 LEMON

1-2 CURRY LEAVES (OPTIONAL)

SALT

TO *GARNISH:*

OMELETTE RINGS (SEE NASI GORENG, PAGE 110)

PRAWN CRACKERS

FRIED ONION RINGS (SEE PAGE 69)

½ CUCUMBER, SLICED VERY THINLY

First make the coconut milk: put the chopped coconut in a measuring jug, pour in boiling water up to the 300 ml (½ pint) mark and stir until the coconut is dissolved. Set aside.

Rinse the rice in a sieve under cold running water, then set aside. Heat the wok until hot. Add the oil and heat over a moderate heat until hot. Add the onions and garlic and stir-fry for 1-2 minutes or until softened, taking care not to let them brown. Add the rice and stir to coat in the oil and onion mixture, then pour in the coconut milk and 600 ml (1 pint) water. Add the turmeric, lemon grass or lemon rind, curry leaves (if using) and salt to taste, stir carefully to mix and bring to the boil. Turn the heat down to its lowest setting, cover the wok with a lid and cook over a very gentle heat for 15 minutes, stirring frequently. If the mixture becomes too thick and starts to stick to the bottom of the wok, add a little water. Remove the wok from the heat and leave to stand, without lifting the lid, for 20-30 minutes. Meanwhile, prepare the garnish ingredients.

To serve, mound the rice on a warmed serving platter and arrange the garnish over and around, grouping the different types of ingredients together. Serve at once.

Serves 4 as a main dish, 6 as part of an oriental meal

PANSIT

This dish is from the Philippines, where it is usually referred to by its full name of 'pancit guisado', meaning 'fried noodles'. All of the ingredients are easy to obtain, apart from nam pla (fish sauce), which can only be bought in specialist oriental stores. If you have difficulty in finding it, use 2 teaspoons anchovy essence instead, although the flavour of the finished dish will not be quite so authentic.

250 G (8 OZ) THREAD OR FINE EGG NOODLES

3 TABLESPOONS VEGETABLE OIL

2 MEDIUM ONIONS, SLICED THINLY

2 CLOVES GARLIC, CRUSHED

250 G (8 OZ) PEELED COOKED PRAWNS, DEFROSTED AND

DRIED THOROUGHLY, IF FROZEN

2 COOKED BONELESS CHICKEN BREASTS, SKINNED AND CUT

INTO THIN STRIPS

1 LARGE THICK SLICE OF COOKED HAM, WEIGHING ABOUT

125 G (4 OZ), CUT INTO THIN STRIPS

150 ML (¼ PINT) FISH STOCK (SEE PAGE 29) OR FISH OR

CHICKEN STOCK MADE FROM A CUBE

4 TABLESPOONS SOY SAUCE

2 TABLESPOONS NAM PLA (FISH SAUCE)

125 G (4 OZ) BEAN SPROUTS

EXTRA SOY SAUCE TO SERVE (OPTIONAL)

TO GARNISH:

LARGE PRAWNS IN THEIR SHELLS

SPRING ONIONS

LIME OR LEMON WEDGES

Cook the noodles according to packet instructions. Drain well, place in a bowl and sprinkle over 1 tablespoon of the oil. Toss to coat, cover and set aside.

Heat the wok until hot. Add the remaining oil and heat over a moderate heat until hot. Add the onions and garlic and stir-fry for 1-2 minutes or until softened, taking care not to let them brown.

Add the prawns, chicken and ham, increase the heat to high and toss to mix, then add the stock, soy sauce and nam pla and stir-fry for 2-3 minutes. Add the bean sprouts and noodles and toss for 1-2 minutes longer or until all the ingredients are combined and piping hot. Serve at once, garnished with prawns in their shells, spring onions and lime or lemon wedges. Hand extra soy sauce separately, for those who like it.

Serves 4 as a main dish

CHAP CHEE

This Korean noodle dish is very simple and quick to cook.
Try to cut the strips of steak as thinly as you can, and slice
the leeks and carrots into the finest possible shreds.

250 G (8 OZ) FILLET OR RUMP STEAK, CUT INTO THIN STRIPS

ACROSS THE GRAIN

250 G (8 OZ) VERMICELLI

10-15 G (¼-½ OZ) DRIED SHIITAKE MUSHROOMS, SOAKED IN

WARM WATER FOR 20 MINUTES

2 TABLESPOONS VEGETABLE OIL

2 MEDIUM LEEKS, SHREDDED

2 MEDIUM CARROTS, SHREDDED

SALT AND PEPPER

MARINADE:

2 TABLESPOONS SOY SAUCE

1 TABLESPOON SESAME OIL

1 CLOVE GARLIC, CRUSHED

First make the marinade: mix all the marinade ingredients together in a shallow dish, add the beef and turn to coat. Cover and set aside for about 20 minutes

Meanwhile, place the vermicelli in a saucepan, cover with boiling water, put on the saucepan lid and leave to soak for 10 minutes. Drain well, then cut the vermicelli into 5-7.5 cm (2-3 inch) lengths.

Drain the mushrooms and reserve the soaking liquid. Slice the mushrooms thinly.

Heat the wok until hot. Add the oil and heat over a moderate heat until hot. Add the beef and its marinade, increase the heat to high and stir-fry for 3-4 minutes or until browned on all sides. Add the leeks, carrots and sliced mushrooms and stir-fry for 2-3 minutes longer, then add the vermicelli and the reserved mushroom soaking liquid. Toss until all the ingredients are combined and piping hot. Add salt and pepper to taste and serve at once.

Serves 2-3 as a supper or lunch dish

ANGEL'S HAIR WITH PRAWNS

Angel's hair is a very thin, long vermicelli, called capelli
d'angelo *in Italian. You can buy it in Italian delicatessens*
and some large supermarkets.

250 G (8 OZ) ANGEL'S HAIR PASTA

3 TABLESPOONS VEGETABLE OIL

4 SPRING ONIONS, SLICED THINLY ON THE DIAGONAL

5 CM (2 INCH) PIECE FRESH ROOT GINGER, PEELED AND

CHOPPED FINELY

2 CLOVES GARLIC, CRUSHED

375 G (12 OZ) RAW 'TIGER' PRAWN TAILS, DEFROSTED AND

DRIED THOROUGHLY, IF FROZEN, PEELED

3 TABLESPOONS DRY SHERRY

90 ML (3 FL OZ) DOUBLE CREAM

3 TABLESPOONS FINELY CHOPPED FLAT LEAF PARSLEY

SALT AND PEPPER

Cook the angel's hair in boiling salted water for 3 minutes, or according to packet instructions. Drain well, place in a bowl and sprinkle over 1 tablespoon of the oil. Toss to coat, cover and set aside.

Heat the wok until hot. Add the remaining oil and heat over a moderate heat until hot. Add the spring onions, ginger and garlic and stir-fry for 30 seconds to just flavour the oil, then add the raw prawns and stir-fry for 1-2 minutes or until they turn pink.

Pour in the sherry and cream, add a little salt and plenty of black pepper, then increase the heat to high and toss to combine. Add the pasta and toss again until the pasta is piping hot. Remove from the heat and sprinkle over the chopped parsley. Serve at once.

Serves 3-4 as a main dish

EXOTIC RICE WITH COCONUT DRESSING

The addition of pineapple to this spicy hot rice dish has a cooling effect; the coconut dressing is the perfect complement.

250 G (8 OZ) LONG-GRAIN RICE

2 TABLESPOONS VEGETABLE OIL

1 SMALL ONION, CHOPPED FINELY

2.5 CM (1 INCH) PIECE FRESH ROOT GINGER, PEELED AND CHOPPED FINELY

1 CLOVE GARLIC, CRUSHED

1 TEASPOON HOT CHILLI POWDER, OR TO TASTE

2 CELERY STICKS, CHOPPED FINELY

1 x 227G (8 OZ) CAN PINEAPPLE IN NATURAL JUICE, DRAINED AND CUT INTO BITE-SIZED PIECES WITH 4 TABLESPOONS JUICE RESERVED

75 G (3 OZ) UNSALTED PEANUTS, CHOPPED ROUGHLY

4 TABLESPOONS CHOPPED FRESH CORIANDER

SALT AND PEPPER

TOASTED SHREDDED OR DESICCATED COCONUT TO GARNISH

COCONUT DRESSING:

100 G (3½ OZ) CREAMED COCONUT, CHOPPED ROUGHLY

2 TABLESPOONS SOY SAUCE

FINELY GRATED RIND AND JUICE OF 1 LIME

PINCH OF SUGAR

Cook the rice in boiling salted water according to packet instructions.

Meanwhile, make the coconut dressing: put the chopped coconut in a measuring jug and stir in boiling water up to the 300 ml (½ pint) mark. Add the soy sauce, lime rind and juice and the sugar. Stir well and set aside.

Drain the rice and set aside. Heat the wok until hot. Add the oil and heat over a moderate heat until hot. Add the onion, ginger, garlic and chilli powder and stir-fry for 2-3 minutes or until softened slightly. Add the cooked rice, celery, pineapple and the reserved juice and peanuts, increase the heat to high and toss until all the ingredients are combined.

Remove the wok from the heat, sprinkle over the chopped coriander, pour over the dressing and toss well to mix. Add salt and pepper to taste and serve hot, warm or cold, sprinkled with toasted coconut.

Serves 4 as an accompaniment

HOW TO SKIN TOMATOES

TOMATO SKIN IS BOTH UNPALATABLE AND UNATTRACTIVE IN STIR-FRIES, YET IT ONLY TAKES A FEW MINUTES TO REMOVE.

TO SKIN A FEW TOMATOES: PIERCE THEM ONE AT A TIME THROUGH THE STALK END WITH THE TINES OF A FORK AND HOLD OVER A GAS FLAME, TURNING THE TOMATO CONSTANTLY UNTIL THE SKIN BLISTERS AND BURSTS.

LEAVE FOR A FEW MOMENTS UNTIL COOL ENOUGH TO HANDLE, THEN STRIP OFF THE SKIN WITH YOUR FINGERS.

QUICK & EASY

IN THIS CHAPTER YOU WILL FIND RECIPES COMBINING STORECUPBOARD AND FROZEN FOODS WITH FRESH INGREDIENTS TO MAKE TASTY DISHES IN NEXT TO NO TIME. IDEAS FOR SUPPERS, SNACKS AND MIDWEEK MEALS THAT TEMPT YOUR TASTEBUDS NO MATTER HOW SIMPLE THEY ARE.

ORIENTAL STIR-FRIED BEEF WITH VEGETABLES

ABOUT 50 G (2 OZ) FLAKED ALMONDS

3 TABLESPOONS VEGETABLE OIL

375-500 G (12 OZ-1 LB) 'FLASH-FRY' OR 'QUICK-GRILL'
STEAK, CUT INTO THIN STRIPS

250 G (8 OZ) PACKET COLESLAW MIX

125 G (4 OZ) BEAN SPROUTS

½ X 160 G (5½ OZ) BOTTLE 'STIR-FRY' BLACK BEAN SAUCE

SALT AND PEPPER

Heat the wok until hot. Add the almonds and dry-fry over a gentle heat until toasted. Remove the wok from the heat and tip the almonds into a bowl. Set aside.

Return the wok to a moderate heat. Add 2 tablespoons of the oil and heat until hot. Add the beef, increase the heat to high and stir-fry for 2-3 minutes or until browned on all sides. Remove the wok from the heat and tip the contents into a bowl.

Return the wok to a moderate heat, add the remaining oil and heat until hot. Add the coleslaw mix and the bean sprouts, increase the heat to high and stir-fry for 2-3 minutes. Return the beef and its juices to the wok, add the black bean sauce and toss until all the ingredients are combined and piping hot. Add salt and pepper to taste and serve at once, sprinkled with the toasted flaked almonds.

Serves 3-4 as a main dish

HAM AND SWEETCORN CHOW MEIN

1 X 250 G (8.82 OZ) PACKET MEDIUM EGG NOODLES

4 TABLESPOONS WATER

2 TABLESPOONS OYSTER SAUCE

1 TABLESPOON VEGETABLE OIL

3-4 SPRING ONIONS, SLICED THINLY ON THE DIAGONAL

1 X 113 G (4 OZ) PACKET SLICED HAM, CUT INTO STRIPS

1 X 198 G (7 OZ) CAN SWEETCORN KERNELS, DRAINED

SALT AND PEPPER

Place the noodles in a pan of boiling water, cover and leave to stand for 6 minutes, according to packet instructions.

Meanwhile, mix the water in a jug or bowl with the oyster sauce. Set aside.

Heat the wok until hot. Add the oil and heat over a moderate heat until hot. Add the spring onions and stir-fry for 30 seconds. Pour in the water and oyster sauce, add the ham and sweetcorn and increase the heat to high. Stir-fry for 1-2 minutes or until hot. Remove the wok from the heat.

Drain the noodles quickly and add to the wok. Return the wok to a high heat and toss until all the ingredients are combined. Add salt and pepper to taste and serve at once.

Serves 2-3 as a main dish

QUICK STIR-FRIED VEGETABLES IN SWEET AND SOUR SAUCE

Packets of ready-prepared 'Chinese-style' vegetables are available at many large supermarkets. They are ideal for stir-frying as they take all of the hard work out of the preparation of the vegetables. The most commonly used vegetables are bean sprouts, red and green peppers, baby corn, mangetout and mushrooms, but ingredients vary from one packet to another.

2 TABLESPOONS VEGETABLE OIL

2 x 250 G (8 OZ) PACKETS CHINESE-STYLE VEGETABLES

1 x 160 G (5½ OZ) BOTTLE 'STIR-FRY' SWEET AND SOUR SAUCE

50 G (2 OZ) UNSALTED ROASTED PEANUTS OR CASHEW NUTS

SALT AND PEPPER

Heat the wok until hot. Add the oil and heat over a moderate heat until hot. Add the vegetables, increase the heat to high and stir-fry for 3-4 minutes or just until beginning to soften.

Add the sweet and sour sauce and toss for 1-2 minutes or until combined with the vegetables and piping hot. Add the nuts and toss to mix, then taste and add salt and pepper if necessary. Serve at once.

Serves 3-4 as an accompaniment, 2-3 as a vegetarian main dish with rice

TEN-MINUTE CHINESE CHICKEN

This simple dish takes a total of 10 minutes preparation and cooking time.

1 TABLESPOON VEGETABLE OIL

4 SKINNED AND BONED CHICKEN BREASTS, EACH WEIGHING ABOUT 150 G (5 OZ), CUT INTO THIN STRIPS ACROSS THE GRAIN

1 x 160 G (5½ OZ) BOTTLE 'STIR-FRY' YELLOW BEAN SAUCE

1 x 300 G (10 OZ) CAN SLICED BUTTON MUSHROOMS IN BRINE, WELL DRAINED

FRESH CORIANDER SPRIGS TO GARNISH (OPTIONAL)

Heat the wok until hot. Add the oil and heat over a moderate heat until hot. Add the chicken strips, increase the heat to high and stir-fry for 3-4 minutes or until the chicken is lightly coloured on all sides.

Add the yellow bean sauce and mushrooms and toss for 1-2 minutes or until all the ingredients are combined and piping hot. Serve at once, garnished with fresh coriander sprigs if liked.

Serves 3-4 as a main dish

PRAWN AND SWEETCORN RISOTTO

Packets of savoury rice come in different varieties according to their brand, so you can ring the changes as often as you please. Ham or chicken can be used instead of the prawns, and frozen peas instead of, or as well as, the sweetcorn.

1 x 125 G (4.4 OZ) PACKET MUSHROOM SAVOURY RICE

450 ML (¾ PINT) WATER

250 G (8 OZ) FROZEN SWEETCORN KERNELS

200 G (7 OZ) PEELED COOKED PRAWNS, DEFROSTED AND

DRIED THOROUGHLY, IF FROZEN

15 G (½ OZ) BUTTER

SALT AND PEPPER

LEMON WEDGES TO SERVE

Put the savoury rice in the wok, add the water and bring to the boil, stirring. Reduce the heat to low, cover with a lid and simmer for 10 minutes.

Add the frozen sweetcorn and simmer for a further 5 minutes, then add the prawns and butter and simmer for a further 5 minutes or until all the liquid is absorbed, stirring occasionally. Add salt and pepper to taste. Serve hot, with lemon wedges.

Serves 2

CHILLI BEEF

Bottled chilli sauce can be found in most large supermarkets as well as oriental stores. The amount you use depends on the brand – some are far hotter than others – and your own personal taste of course. Silken tofu is sold at health food shops; it is not essential for this dish, but it does add extra protein.

2 TABLESPOONS VEGETABLE OIL

1 BUNCH SPRING ONIONS, CHOPPED ROUGHLY

375 G (12 OZ) MINCED BEEF

300 ML (½ PINT) BEEF STOCK MADE FROM A CUBE

2 TABLESPOONS BLACK BEAN SAUCE

2 TABLESPOONS CHILLI SAUCE OR TO TASTE

1 TEASPOON DARK SOFT BROWN SUGAR

1 x 297 G (10.5 OZ) PACKET SILKEN TOFU (BEAN CURD),

DRAINED AND DICED

SALT

Heat the wok until hot. Add the oil and heat over a moderate heat until hot. Add half of the spring onions and stir-fry for 1-2 minutes or until softened slightly, taking care not to let them brown. Add the beef, increase the heat to high and stir-fry for 3-4 minutes or until browned on all sides, pressing well to remove any lumps in the meat.

Add the beef stock, black bean and chilli sauces and brown sugar and bring to the boil, stirring. Lower the heat, cover the wok with a lid and cook for 10-15 minutes or until the beef mixture is reduced and thickened, stirring frequently.

Add the tofu and stir in gently. Heat through, then taste and add salt if necessary. Serve at once, sprinkled with the remaining chopped spring onions.

Serves 4 as a main dish

SZECHUAN PEPPER CHICKEN

Szechuan dishes are often hot and spicy. This recipe uses bottled chilli sauce to create instant heat. You can add more than suggested here if you like, taking into account the 'hotness' of the brand you are using. To save time crushing garlic, you could use 1 teaspoon garlic purée or ½ teaspoon garlic salt instead.

4 TABLESPOONS WATER

2 TABLESPOONS BOTTLED HOT CHILLI SAUCE, OR TO TASTE

1 TABLESPOON SOY SAUCE

2 TABLESPOONS VEGETABLE OIL

3-4 SPRING ONIONS, SLICED THINLY ON THE DIAGONAL

5 CM (2 INCH) PIECE FRESH ROOT GINGER, PEELED AND CHOPPED FINELY

1 CLOVE GARLIC, CRUSHED

4 SKINNED AND BONED CHICKEN BREASTS, EACH WEIGHING ABOUT 150 G (5 OZ), CUT INTO THIN STRIPS ACROSS THE GRAIN

SPRING ONIONS TO GARNISH (OPTIONAL)

Mix the water in a jug or bowl with the hot chilli sauce and soy sauce. Set aside.

Heat the wok until hot. Add the oil and heat over a moderate heat until hot. Add the spring onions, ginger and garlic and stir-fry for 30 seconds. Add the chicken strips, increase the heat to high and stir-fry for 3-4 minutes or until lightly coloured on all sides.

Add the chilli sauce mixture and toss until all the ingredients are well combined and piping hot. Serve at once, garnished with spring onions if liked.

Serves 3-4 as a main dish

THREE-BEAN STIR-FRY

This clever recipe uses bottled salad dressing to both cook and flavour canned pulses. The choice of salad dressings available is enormous and you can ring the changes as you wish, but 'garlic and herb dressing' is particularly good with beans because it has a strong flavour, so too is 'Italian dressing', although this may not contain garlic.

5 TABLESPOONS BOTTLED GARLIC AND HERB DRESSING

2 CELERY STICKS, SLICED THINLY ON THE DIAGONAL

1 MEDIUM ONION, SLICED THINLY

1 x 425 G (15.2 OZ) CAN RED KIDNEY BEANS, DRAINED AND RINSED

1 x 432 G (15.2 OZ) CAN CHICK PEAS, DRAINED AND RINSED

1 x 400 G (14 OZ) CAN CANNELLINI BEANS, DRAINED AND RINSED

SALT AND PEPPER

TO GARNISH:

CHOPPED FRESH HERBS

FINELY CHOPPED GARLIC

Heat the wok until hot. Add 2 tablespoons of the dressing and heat over a moderate heat until hot. Add the celery and onion and stir-fry for 2-3 minutes or until softened, taking care not to let them brown.

Add all the beans and the remaining dressing, increase the heat to high and stir-fry for 2-3 minutes or until most of the liquid has evaporated and the ingredients are piping hot. Add salt and pepper to taste and serve at once, sprinkled with chopped fresh herbs and garlic.

Serves 3-4 as a vegetarian main dish, with rice or bread as an accompaniment

INDEX

ACKNOWLEDGEMENTS

Editor: Nicola Hill
Art Editor: Sarah Pollock
Photographer: James Murphy
Home Economist: Allyson Birch
Stylist: Róisín Nield
Line Illustration: Jared Gilbey

AUTHOR'S ACKNOWLEDGEMENT

*With grateful thanks to Mary Pope,
for her help with testing the recipes*